Centerville Library
Washington-Centerville Public Library
Centerville, Ohio

HAIR

HAIR:
FASHION

**LAURENT
PHILIPPON**

AND

FANTASY

Thames & Hudson

Title page:
Blonde Venus – Julie Delpy.
Hair by Laurent Philippon.
Photo Pierre et Gilles 1992
Right: Girls applying
for a hair modelling job.
Photo Thomas McAvoy

Hair: Fashion and Fantasy ©
2013 Thames & Hudson Ltd,
London

Text © Laurent Philippon and
the contributing authors

All Rights Reserved. No part
of this publication may be
reproduced or transmitted in
any form or by any means,
electronic or mechanical,
including photocopy, recording
or any other information storage
and retrieval system, without
prior permission in writing from
the publisher.

First published in 2013 in
paperback in the United States
of America by Thames & Hudson
Inc., 500 Fifth Avenue,
New York, New York 10110

thamesandhudsonusa.com

Library of Congress Catalog
Card Number 2012956282

ISBN 978-0-500-29108-5

Printed and bound in China by
C&C Offset Printing Co. Ltd

PREFACE

I am on a constant search for inspiration. Art, cinema, travelling to different cities, people-watching... I absorb everything I can about our everyday visual world. This book has extended my appetite: for almost ten years I have visited libraries, museums and bookshops wherever I have found myself, on a quest for knowledge about the art of hair. It is a living art, as wide, vast and varied as the people who wear their hair in every conceivable style, from the slickest city streets to distant villages in Africa.

I have been inspired by the idea that our ancestors performed the most sophisticated and refined hairstyling using sometimes the most primitive techniques. Occasionally this can be conveyed in pictures, but sometimes I have discovered extraordinary and rare treasures by hairdressers who remain anonymous, and some of these are truly thrilling.

Our individuality – how we wear our clothes, define our group, or say who we are – depends on how we wear our hair. Artists have used hair as a medium, not just for the sake of beautification, but to reveal the beauty of hair itself, and the creative spirit that moves us.

I have had the opportunity to assist the greatest masters of our time: Alexandre de Paris, Julien d'Ys, Orlando Pita, Yannick d'Is and Sam McKnight have all given me the honour of learning at their side. These exceptional and passionate people have lifted their art to a new level of refinement. They have taught and influenced me so much, and it is thanks to their generosity and talent that I have tried to understand the language and poetry of hair.

I respectfully dedicate this book to them, and to inspirational unknown hairstylists everywhere.

OPPOSITE
Hair by Laurent Philippon.
Photo Norbert Schoerner
2007

THE ART OF HAIR

What is beauty?

It is subjective and yet at the same time there for all to see. The beauty of a hairstyle speaks for itself: anyone with a curious eye can understand a hairstyle. Whether it is Assyrian curls, African braids or a Chinese chignon, hair crowns the human body. Every culture and fashion carries different codes, but hairstyles have a kind of universality.

Throughout history, hairstyles have conferred status on their wearer. In ancient Egypt, Cleopatra wore elaborate braids. In 18th-century France, Marie Antoinette's contemporaries competed to pile their hair outrageously high. Roman centurions wore feathered plumes, and so did Native American 'Mohawk' warriors, in turn echoed by street styles of anarchists and punks in 1970s London and New York. Fashion and status are forever linked.

As with all kinds of art and adornment, there is a constant exchange of ideas between high fashion and popular reality. Today's instant communication networks transmit the looks of fashion celebrities, pop stars and style leaders to anywhere in the world, and a global variety of responses are beamed right back. The result can mean local traditions and styles are lost in the flood of globalized fashions.

It is not only chieftains, empresses and anarchists who have expressed their status via their hair. Hair carries strong spiritual symbolism, both in Eastern and Western religions, perhaps being the closest part of us to heaven. Monks and spiritual devotees everywhere show their calling by varying the length, pattern or style of their hair.

OPPOSITE
Laurent Philippon (left)
and Alexandre Raimon
(Alexandre de Paris),
with Laetitia Scherrer.
Photo Cédric Dordevic
1991

The way hair is worn – modestly veiled, preciously adorned, or free to the wind – can give an aura of great intimacy and sensuality. Loose hair was considered a sign of great beauty in Japan in the 8th and 9th centuries, but it was taboo for women in some Catholic countries to wear their hair loose even recently.

Hair is the one part of our body that we can change whenever we want, without causing any permanent damage. We can dress it up or dress it down, to reflect our personality, to attract attention, to project a chosen identity or to seize the mood of the moment. In fact, hair is a sort of identity card that gives information about a person. In some parts of Africa, it is possible to 'read' the story of someone's life by paying close attention to their hairstyle.

Hairdressing is part of the way we beautify ourselves. History has witnessed an abundance of different styles, and hairstyling is a genuine art form: it symbolically represents our transition from unkempt barbarians to civilized social beings. We are the only animals on the planet to give our hair so much care and attention.

Inspiration is everywhere: history, cinema, art, photography and fashion provide constant sources of ideas, examples and models. In fashion photography, hairstyling is often the most versatile and sophisticated way to set the tone of the whole shoot. The style of hair can alter the mood and effect, whether glamorous or sensuous, formal or relaxed, still or frenzied. Hairstyles bring fashion to life.

The book has been put together according to individual styles, including examples from every age and variety of human culture. Each chapter opens with an introductory sweep across the horizon, looking at historical figures, the world of artists' imagination and civilizations around the globe. Taking these sources as inspiration, I have compiled a series of some of the best fashion photographs I have seen from friends, colleagues, mentors and the finest available archives today. Each shows an essential hairstyle in a unique or definitive way. The most intricate braids; the most expressive loose, free-flowing hair; the most sophisticated chignons; the wildest wigs; the coolest or trashiest blonds...

Photographers, stylists, artists, models and commentators all have a say here, in a collection of treasures and surprises. This book is, of course, a personal journey for me, but I hope it will bring these many voices together, all with ideas to share and inspiration to lift our creative spirits.

B
R
A
/
D
S

14

1.

2.

3.

1.
Indian *sadhu* (holy man).
For this Hindu follower
of Vishnu, his *jata*
(dreadlocks) show
his disregard for human
vanity, but they may
also symbolize potency.

considered a traitor and
was liable to be executed.
As the saying went:
'Keep your hair and lose
your head, or keep your
head and cut your hair.'

2.
Cutting off a man's braid,
China, 1912. At the end
of the Qing dynasty, the
tradition for men to wear
their hair in a long plait
was outlawed. Anyone
who didn't cut it off was

3.
Tibetan girls undergo
a change of hairstyle as
part of an initiation rite
before marriage. Up to
108 strands are plaited
into a special braid
(108 is a sacred number
in Buddhism).

BRAIDING is one of the oldest ways of styling hair known to us. Probably inspired by the process of weaving together strands of straw, or wool, rush or horsehair to make textiles, ropes and other items for practical use, it requires no special instrument or tool and can be worked simply using the fingers. Any type of hair can be braided, whether it is straight, curly or frizzy.

Of great practical use for keeping hair out of the eyes, especially while working, the braid has given rise to expressions of boundless creativity and inventiveness. It has carried all sorts of coded messages, providing information, sometimes in a very beautiful and poetic fashion, about the person wearing it. Countless different methods of braiding have been invented over the centuries. The classic style is the three-strand plait, but hair can also be braided using four, five or six strands, or even woven from as many as twenty separate sections.

The variety of different patterns that can be achieved is infinite. Some examples include the fishtail braid, which can be seen in ancient Egyptian paintings; the 'corn row', which enables different designs to be created close to the scalp, as in Africa; the twisted braid, which was very fashionable in Europe in the 18th century; and so-called French braids, which were widely fashionable during the Italian Renaissance. Decorative items, such as flowers or even jewelry, can also be attached using this technique.

Today, the braid continues to be endlessly popular. Innovative braiding styles compete with each other in the world of fashion and in everyday life, and are the basis of an extensive range of hair-styles. In African communities around the world, 'braiding sessions' are social occasions, and can attract crowds of participants and onlookers, with one or more people having their hair transformed into wonderful new braided creations of huge variety and ingenuity.

PREVIOUS PAGES
Marc Jacobs (left), Laurent
Philippon, Naomi Campbell.
Hair by Laurent Philippon.
Photo Jean-Paul Goude
2007

OPPOSITE
Mexican artist Frida Kahlo wore her hair in a distinctive personal style, with two braids interlaced with ribbons and tied in a crown on top of the head, which she then decorated with flowers, combs, feathers or jewelry. Politically engaged all her life, she proudly celebrated her mixed German-Amerindian family origins.

ABOVE
Roots of Life. Photo Mote Sinabel Aoki. Women of the Himba tribe of Namibia wear their hair in braids that are treated daily with otjize paste, a mixture of butter, red ochre, herbs and resin. The aromatic red paste protects hair from the sun, but is also a cosmetic designed for seduction. The rich colour, like the fertile Namibian earth, is a symbol of life.

1.
Wheatpaste collage by street artists the Paper Twins. Photo Mike Germon, 2010

2.
Reggae star Bob Marley (shown here playing live in 1979) is probably the best-known wearer of dreadlocks. He grew them as part of his Rastafarian beliefs. Dreadlocks were popularized by the Jamaican leader of the 'Youth Black Faith' movement, Bongo Watto, in 1949. Some say the name comes from 'dreadful locks', meaning either the wearer looked dreadful or was to be dreaded. Some wearers consider their dreadlocks sacred, others a source of strength, or a symbolic sign of rebellion against oppression.

3.
Twenty-stranded braid, Fraga, Spain 1930

2.

1.

3.

4.

5.

6.

4.
Braid patterns, 19th century. After the French Revolution, no one wanted to be seen to be an 'aristocrat' – to wear towering hair like Marie Antoinette's would be a dangerous personal fashion statement. For years after the Revolution hair was worn in simple, severe styles. In the 1820s Parisian hairdresser Ambroise Croizat made more intricate hairstyles fashionable again, creating dozens of braid patterns such as these for some of the most famous coiffures of his age. 'Fashion only exists in Paris,' he declared, 'that is where all the world's most elegant hairstyles begin.'

5.
Renaissance beauty took inspiration from nature: the regular patterns found in ears of corn or snake scales were echoed in the intricate coiled braids fashionable during the 15th and 16th centuries in Italy.

6.
Leda by Leonardo da Vinci, c. 1506

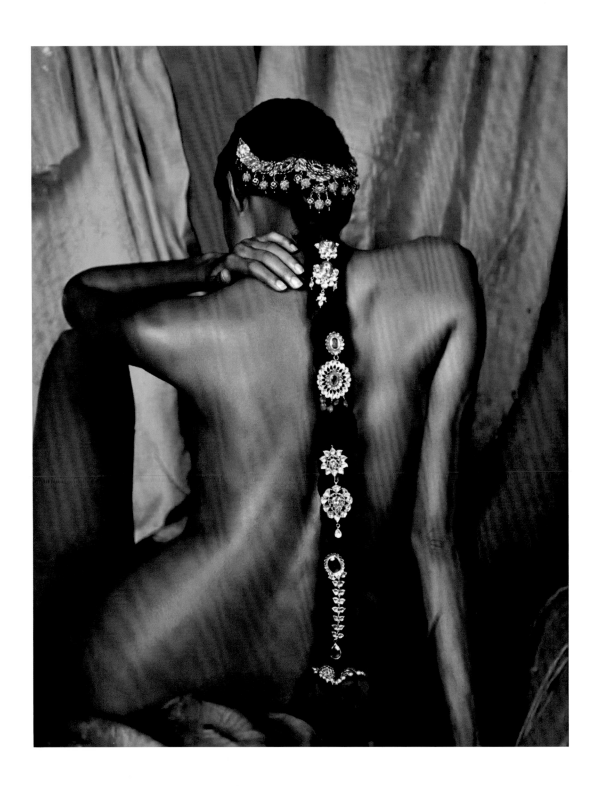

OPPOSITE
Indian women wear
a long plaited braid that
follows the movements
of the back in harmony
with the energy of the
chakras, or centres
of vital energy, common
to Hindu and Buddhist
traditions. Hair by Deepa
Verma. Photo Prabuddha
Dasgupta
2007

ABOVE
Hotel Kanaga, Mopti,
Mali. Katoucha Niane
and Djimon Hounsou.
Hair by Sally. Photo
Thierry Mugler
1989

1.

1.
Sango people, Congo Free State (present-day Democratic Republic of the Congo), central Africa, 1905

2.

2. *HAWOYE KAÏDIAGADA*

In the magnificent mud-brick commune of Djenné, Mali, lives a woman whose fame for her braiding skills is legendary. Hawoye Kaïdiagada is respected not only for her hairstyling talents but also for her gift of augury (interpreting signs).

Young women travel from far away, often on foot, to have their hair braided by her, especially for important weddings. She works sitting on the ground in her house, strictly observing the traditional ancestral codes.

Hairstyles are considered as identity cards in most regions of Africa. Hawoye knows the traditions relating to hair better than almost anyone else. She holds conversations with each new customer before a braiding session in order to establish which are the motifs most appropriate to the wearer's status.

After the work of braiding is finished, Hawoye strokes the hair with a flaming twist of cloth soaked in shea butter to burn away stray hairs, and to ward off evil spirits. Photo Cédric Dordevic, 2010

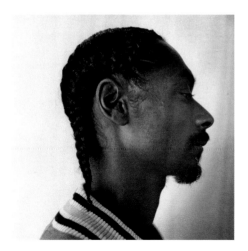

3.

4.

5.

3.
Rapper Snoop Dogg,
2003

4.
Braid paintings by So Yoon
Lym, 2009/2010. The
artist says: 'These braid
patterns are the language
for the new aboriginal,
the transplanted and
deterritorialized nomad...
he wears his location like
an image-text on his head.'

5. *AFRICAN BRAIDS*

Intricate braids, beads and ceremonial
ornamentation: an African chieftain portrayed
in a 19th-century engraving.

Hairstyles have always held an important
place in African culture. Often information
can be conveyed through a hairstyle, such
as social status, age, religion, ethnic identity
and occupation.

At the beginning of the 16th century,
Europeans initiated a slave trade that would
endure for over four hundred years. The peoples
of West Africa, notably from the countries today
known as Senegal, Gambia, Sierra Leone,
Ghana and Nigeria, were particularly exploited.
Their hair was routinely shaved off, effacing
the most visible sign of cultural distinction.
Men and women were rendered anonymous.

As conditions became slightly less brutal
in the 18th-century Americas, some slave
owners granted their slaves Sunday off. One of
the first occupations that was revived on this
precious day of rest was to style hair, to reclaim
some individual identity. Without access to the
unguents they had once traditionally applied,
ingenuity provided butter, wax and other
substances to help shape the hair.

ABOVE
Elizabeth Taylor in
Cleopatra, directed by
Joseph L. Mankiewicz.
Hair by Alexandre de Paris
1963

OPPOSITE
Bo Derek in *10*, directed
by Blake Edwards. Hair by
Mary Keats. Photo Bruce
McBroom
1979

LEFT
Hair by Laurent Philippon.
Photo David Marvier
2011

OPPOSITE
Hair by Laurent Philippon.
Photo Norbert Schoerner
2007

LAURENT PHILIPPON
TALKS TO SHOPLIFTER

SHOPLIFTER (aka Hrafnhildur Arnardóttir) is an artist born in Iceland and living in New York.

OPPOSITE
Björk, in a photo taken for the sleeve of her album *Medúlla*. Hair sculpture by Shoplifter. Photo Inez van Lamsweerde and Vinoodh Matadin 2004

LAURENT PHILIPPON: Your art pieces are so detailed and the craftsmanship is admirable. It must take forever to create them. Do you do the braiding yourself, or do you have a team of braiders?

SHOPLIFTER: I can't do the braiding by myself any more on these projects; I have people to help. I would prefer to do it myself, but it's too time-consuming. I have an army of braiders! I get very obsessive about the way the braids should be: not too tight, because I like to bend them, but not too loose or they come apart. Newcomers must sometimes think I'm crazy!

LP: They're not just simple braids; they're taken to another dimension. What does hair represent to you?

S: All my work stems from human vanity. People usually see vanity as something negative but I like to celebrate it. I think it brings out the best in us human beings. We try to beautify ourselves out of vanity, and I think there's nothing more amazing than trying to make this world more beautiful, starting with ourselves. Also, hair grows on us, it connects.

LP: I guess the very first braiding – I'm talking about 10,000 years ago – was probably born out of a practical need, to keep the hair away from the face...

S: ...and then somebody did it better than others, creating styles that became more and more intricate. I'm fascinated by the way we use our hairstyle to enforce our identity.

LP: Hair is the only malleable part of our body.

S: The way we wear our hair is a manifestation of who we are as individuals. When I was ten I had long hair. My mum decided to take me to the hairdresser for a haircut. I thought, 'Great!' The hairdresser braided my hair... then chopped off the braid! I felt as though a limb had been amputated. I didn't recognize myself afterwards; I didn't feel pretty. It was a whole new connection with my identity. All kinds of things came out of that experience. The whole point of the braid being cut off was that I would get to keep it. I created a little shrine for it so I could look at it whenever I wanted to.

OPPOSITE
Björk, in a photo taken for the sleeve of her album *Medúlla*. Hair sculpture by Shoplifter. Photo Inez van Lamsweerde and Vinoodh Matadin 2004

LP: You made it into a sacred object?

s: Yes, it was made into a sort of relic. There was something bitter-sweet about that.

LP: You grew up in Iceland. Did you go to art school there?

s: In my neighbourhood there was a kind of experimental school that was more liberal, hippy style. I always picked painting, drawing, sewing and crochet.

LP: Your first art pieces didn't involve hair...

s: No, that came later, after I finished at art school in Reykjavik. At that time I was more focused on painting and drawing. I moved to New York to study at the School of Visual Arts and started to work with different materials in 3D. I started roaming around the dollar stores where they sold synthetic hair extensions, and that gave me the idea of doing hair portraits. I love using braid – I think about the time this hair took to grow and the time it took to braid.

LP: You created incredible braids for Björk. Was this the first time that you created your art on someone's head instead of for a wall in a gallery?

s: Yes! Björk was working on a new album about the human body, and she asked me to contribute to the cover design. We were thinking of something like a woven basket, ornate with memory flowers, which is an old Icelandic craft. The attachment was done on the day of the photo shoot – I made it a little like a flower arrangement. I insisted on taking a picture from the back and it ended up on the back of the album cover. I love the fact that there is no face – it's a hair portrait.

RIGHT
Twiggy, dress by Grès,
hair by Ara Gallant.
Photograph
by Richard Avedon

RIGHT
Untitled no. 25.
RongRong & Inri
2008

ABOVE
The Birthday Party.
Photo Vee Speers
 2007

OPPOSITE
Laetitia Casta.
Hair by Laurent Philippon.
Photo Cédric Buchet
 2009

Nikki Tucker

A CROWN OF BRAIDS

OPPOSITE
Alicia Keys.
Hair by Nikki Tucker.
2002

I learned to braid at my cousin's house in the projects in New Jersey, when I was around thirteen. There was a girl who used to braid everybody's hair in the apartment next door and I used to watch her all the time. I then started to braid myself – I'd force my brothers to sit down so I could practise on them, and anybody else who would let me.

I did Alicia Keys's hair for years, including for the 2001 Grammys party with Clive Davis, before she released her first album – no one really knew who she was then. Her hair is very curly and she didn't want to wear it straightened. I believe it had something to do with her mixed culture and her upbringing in Harlem.

I studied traditional African braided styles at school from Willie L. Morrow's book *400 Years Without a Comb*. I was fascinated by how they used natural elements to adorn their braids and how pretty were all those designs from different tribes for all kinds of ceremonies. For some, braided hair was like a sort of crown. I am of mixed-culture Afro-American and American Indian heritage, so I feel both cultures' influence – but I make it modern.

Braiding is important to me: it is my calling as a black American Indian woman. During slave times, we were not allowed to do anything traditional and our ancestors were forced to cover their hair with a handkerchief or a scarf to hide their braids.

I still press hair, I pincurl it and I braid it. I use only natural products. I have so many bookings because of that. Black women don't know how to take care of their hair any more – they all wear wigs or extensions. I find looks from 1920s, '30s and '50s European hairstyles that I like and then I try to figure out how to do it in a braided style, using their hair – I don't want them to forget that they have hair.

ABOVE
Hair by Laurent Philippon.
Photo Thomas Schenk
2005

OPPOSITE
Hair by Laurent Philippon.
Photo Thiemo Sander
2001

HAIR EVOLUTION

Eugene Souleiman

I loved to draw at an early age. I always had a creative imagination. Today I like the work of the Chapman Brothers because it has a kind of punk spirit to it. I failed miserably at art school – I was in a punk band.

A careers adviser told me I would make a really good hairdresser. She said I could go to college and learn how to make wigs. I was like, 'Wigs? What are wigs?'

So I learned to barber hair, to cut and dress women's hair, and wig-making; I learned the science, and I really enjoyed it. Learning hairdressing was the first time I fell in love with something. I went to work with Trevor Sorbie, who used to be the top guy at Vidal Sassoon. It's probably the best education any hairdresser could have.

Twenty-five years ago the grunge scene happened, and I ended up working for *The Face* and *i-D* magazines. I started to do shows –

Yohji Yamamoto was the first big designer I ever worked for – then Prada. It was easy, it was fun. I didn't even know who Prada were – really!

I'm from southeast London so I'm used to the mixing of cultures and understanding different sensibilities. Today we've become magpies. We live at such a fast pace. A lot of designers work more like stylists. We look at hair now in a very considered way; the lines between masculine and feminine have become blurred. You can do really glamorous hair with a girl in a suit, or you can combine very pretty clothes, like floral prints, with a small head that's more groomed.

You can't look at hair as just hair any more. You have to think in relation to the person, the lifestyle, and do something that's contradictory.

To evolve you have to break a pattern.

OPPOSITE
Hair by Eugene Souleiman.
Photo Richard Bush
2005

C
U
R
L
S

1.

2.

3.

1.
Frans Pourbus the
Younger, *Anne of Austria*,
1616. Pictured here at the
age of fifteen, the newly
married Queen consort
of France was a renowned
beauty. Her hairstyle
'à bouffon' was enhanced
by little ringlets that
fell softly on either side
of the face.

2.
A hairstyle created
for debutantes
for presentation at
court in London in
the 1950s, with space
for plumes to be
clipped into the hair.

3.
Veronica Lake.
Photo c. 1947

CURLS

We have always tried to improve our looks by changing our hair. Our ancestors realized that framing the face with beautiful wavy curls softens and enhances its shape.

Waves of hair flowing abundantly down a woman's back, and the sensuality suggested by richly curled locks, have inspired artists, sculptors and painters through the ages in their quest to portray the idealized female form.

The oldest instruments used for curling hair have been found in the royal tombs of ancient Egypt, dating back over three thousand years. The Assyrians achieved very uniform curls both in their hair and in their beards by applying a metal tube heated over a brazier, a method that remained in use for at least one thousand years, spreading throughout Asia and Europe.

In France the 'papillote' technique (wrapping damp strands of hair with strips of paper) became prized at the beginning of the 17th century thanks to Anne of Austria and her famous 'à bouffon' hairstyle, cascades of soft curls falling on either side of the face.

In the Romantic era – when it was said that 'passion overtook reason' – long curls were tied loosely at the back of the head, with strands floating freely in the breeze. In 1881 Marcel Grateau invented the 'Marcel Wave' with his patented 'curling iron', a success throughout the world and the inspiration of today's electric version. Hollywood hairdressers all used the modern curling tong to lend the glamorous look to the first movie actresses. The permanent wave came later, allowing the creation of a long-lasting curl – and freeing women from endless hours sitting under hairdryers.

In the 1960s and '70s African-Americans wore their hair with pride in its natural state, emphasizing the volume that could be created by tiny curls, and the 'Afro' was born.

PREVIOUS PAGES
Hair by Laurent Philippon.
Photo David LaChapelle
2002

ABOVE
Rita Hayworth
in *Gilda*, 1946.
Hair by Helen Hunt

OPPOSITE
Renée Perle. Photo
Jacques-Henri Lartigue
1931

52

1.

2.

4.

3.

1.
Marisa Berenson
in *Barry Lyndon*, directed
by Stanley Kubrick, 1975.
Wig by Leonard of Mayfair

2.
Paolo Veronese,
*The Mystic Marriage of
St Catherine* (detail),
c. 1575

3.
Elizabeth Taylor and
Alexandre de Paris, 1960s

4.
Alison Arngrim as Nellie
Oleson, *Little House on
the Prairie*. Photo Patrick
Loubatière

5.

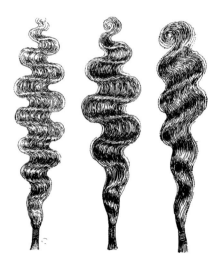

6.

7.

5.
Assyrian men grew their hair and beards long, and used metal tubes heated over coals to curl them. Noblemen would dress their hair with gold dust. Relief from 8th century BC, Sargon Palace in Khorsabad, present-day Iraq.

6.
Marcel Grateau (1852–1936) invented a curling technique using hot irons that gave a beautiful uniform effect, called the 'Marcel Wave'.

7.
Elsa Lanchester in *Bride of Frankenstein*, directed by James Whale, 1935. Hair by Irma Kusely

THE ANALYSIS OF BEAUTY
'The most amiable is the flowing curl; and the many waving and contrasted turns of naturally intermingling locks ravish the eye with the pleasure of the pursuit especially when they are put in motion by a gentle breeze.'
William Hogarth, *The Analysis of Beauty*, 1753

54

RIGHT
Soirée de coiffure.
Photo Brassaï
c. 1930

ABOVE
Bracelet by Boucheron.
Hair by Antoine. Photo
George Hoyningen-Huene
1932

OPPOSITE
Ona Munson as 'Mother'
Gin Sling in *The Shanghai
Gesture*, directed by Josef
von Sternberg. Hair by
Hazel Rogers
1941

BLACK IS BEAUTIFUL

'As a stylist, I like diversity in clothing, jewelry, accessories, make-up and, of course, hair.

'A good Afro has helped me many times to take a fashion story from average to fabulous. Black or platinum blond, hyper-exaggerated or tight and neatly curled... I love a well done 'fro.

'As a black woman, it has personal meaning to me as well. I am thrilled that "black hair" is finally recognized as beautiful, fashionable and desirable.

'Pioneers like Angela Davis, Pam Grier and Melba Tolliver came out as proud black women and showed everyone that an Afro is beautiful. Thanks to them we have more diversity today, which makes this world a more colourful place and my job a bit more fun.'

Patti Wilson

OPPOSITE
Pam Grier in *Foxy Brown*,
directed by Jack Hill
1974

ABOVE
Shalom Harlow.
Hair by Yannick d'Is.
Photo Max Vadukul
1993

OPPOSITE
Julia Stegner. Hair
by Laurent Philippon.
Photo Claudia Knoepfel
and Stefan Indlekofer
2010

Ali Mahdavi
meets Dita Von Teese

RED LIPS, WHITE SKIN,
BLACK HAIR

OPPOSITE
Dita Von Teese.
Hair by Laurent
Philippon. Photo
Ali Mahdavi
2012

I grew up in a small farming town in Michigan. My mother loved to watch old movies so I watched them with her. Betty Grable was probably my biggest hair inspiration. She was blond but her make-up and hairstyle in glorious technicolour continues to fascinate me. I also admired Carmen Miranda and Hedy Lamarr.

I love Marilyn Monroe's hairstyle when she first came to Hollywood – a Marcel-waved bob – and I love Veronica Lake's long waved hairstyle. The erotic bondage drawings of John Willie are also something I've tried to emulate. I love to look at images of Lauren Bacall, Marilyn Monroe and Rita Hayworth and turn them into my own extreme style.

I am naturally blond. When I graduated from high school I started going to underground clubs in Los Angeles. I wore a '60s-style beehive – I was still blond – and a long Barbarella-style ponytail. I got bored of just styling and went bright red in a '50s-style flip. After I went really dark burgundy there was nowhere else to go but black. Wearing dark hair counteracted my shyness. I liked feeling different: it was a form of experimental theatre, my own living work of art. I could wear more make-up which I love – that's when I began to be obsessed with this code of red lips, white skin and black hair.

When I started to be inspired by 1930s and 1940s styles, I would stay home on Friday night and Saturday night and just practise doing my hair. I would even do my hair to go to the grocery store! The more you do something the more you become good at it. I fantasize about going back to my natural blond but I have a fear of it, too – people haven't seen me with my natural blond hair in twenty years.

My biggest fear would be to have to go out with dishevelled, messy, loose, straight hair. That would be against my own code of beauty.

OPPOSITE
Hair by Laurent Philippon.
Photo Sølve Sundsbø
2009

FOLLOWING PAGES
*Dear Doctor, I've Read
Your Play.* Hair by
Laurent Philippon. Photo
David LaChapelle
2004

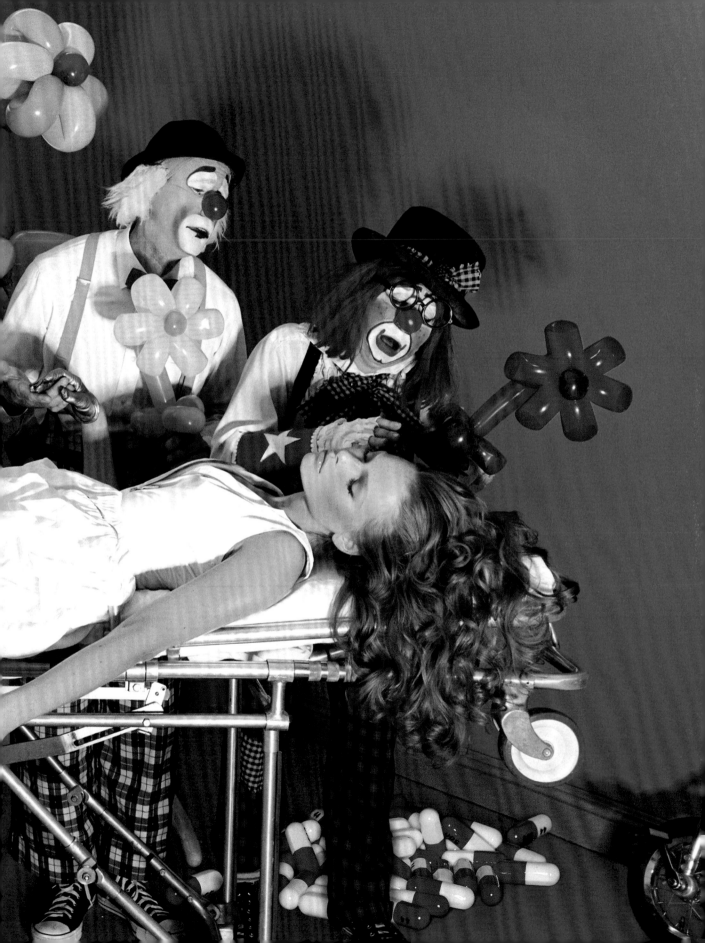

ABOVE
Eva Herzigova. Hair
by Laurent Philippon.
Photo Cédric Buchet
2008

OPPOSITE
Elin Skoghagen. Hair
by Eugene Souleiman.
Photo Greg Kadel
2006

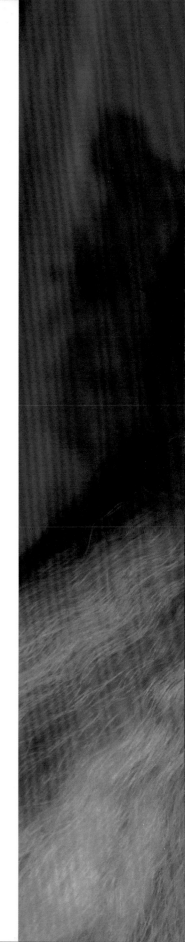

PREVIOUS PAGES
Caroline Trentini and
Orlando Pita. Hair by
Orlando Pita. Photo
Craig McDean
2005

RIGHT
Hair by John at
Leonard of Mayfair.
Photo Barry Lategan
1973

RIGHT
Photo Barry Lategan
1972

76

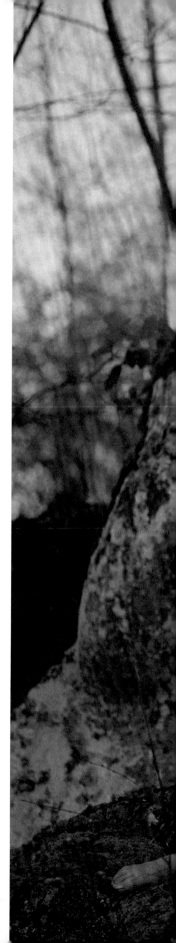

RIGHT
Veruschka in the Park
of Monsters, Bomarzo.
Hair by Alba e Francesca.
Photo Franco Rubartelli
1969

OPPOSITE
Hair by Laurent Philippon.
Photo Bojana Tatarska
2011

LOOSE HAIR

1.

2.

3.

1.
John Lennon and Yoko
Ono hold a 'Bed-In' for
world peace, Amsterdam
Hilton, March 1969

2.
Lucien Lévy-Dhurmer, *Eve*,
1896

3.
At Knebworth Festival,
1979

LOOSE HAIR grows, constantly regenerating itself,

a living protective mane. Hair is a vestige from our animal past: when we tame it with brushes, combs, pins, powders and oils, we mark out our evolution from primitive to civilized being. When we let it down, we set ourselves free.

When we return to our natural state, we lose inhibitions. For many centuries in many societies, hair worn loose has been reserved for moments of intimacy. In some cultures hair is only uncovered in private circumstances. During the Renaissance period, representations of women with loose hair were considered daring or even taboo.

Hair can be an erotic part of us, as intimate as parts of the body that are usually covered. Unveiled hair becomes synonymous with sensuality, freedom and fantasy. In Asia and the Middle East there are variations on an erotic dance style that celebrates unveiled hair.

For women, long loose hair has often been associated with seduction and eroticism; for a man it can also symbolize power and virility. In the Old Testament of the Bible Samson's strength derives from his hair.

During the Heian period in Japan (794–1185), when the imperial court was at its most refined, noble women would grow their hair as long as possible, preferably down to the ground: a cascade of smooth ebony hair was considered the height of beauty. Of course, keeping such treasure well combed, oiled and perfumed was manageable only for women with time and servants to spare.

In the USA during the 1950s long hair for both men and women was associated with the counterculture: it signified the laid-back opposite to the crew-cut and military discipline, the free-thinking alternative to straight-cut, brilliantined, combed and parted styles. In the 1960s and '70s, long loose hair became a way of demonstrating liberation and equality, peace and love.

PREVIOUS PAGES
Hair by Laurent Philippon.
Photo Terry Richardson
2008

1.

2.

3.

4.

1.
Venus rises from the
waves: she freely defies
natural laws, while
appearing as an ideal
of natural perfection.
Alexandre Cabanel,
The Birth of Venus, 1863

2.
Carole Bouquet in
For Your Eyes Only, 1981.
Hair by Stephanie Kaye

3.
Thai girls with 'loose'
beehives in Amsterdam.
Photo Theo van Houts,
1968

4.
John William Waterhouse,
Hylas and the Nymphs,
1896. Hylas was a young
companion to Hercules.
Together they joined the
Argonauts on the quest
for the Golden Fleece.
When Hylas went to
collect water he was
abducted by nymphs
and was never seen
again. Hercules wept,
heartbroken. The nymphs'
faces look innocent, but
their loose red hair hints
at their dangerously
free and seductive spirit.

FOLLOWING PAGES
Wuthering Heights.
Hair by Laurent Philippon.
Photo Duane Michals
2000

THE FARRAH FLIP

Farrah Fawcett starred in the classic 1970s
TV series *Charlie's Angels*.

More memorably, however, she possessed
quite simply the most famous hairstyle
of the era: her golden blond highlights were
skilfully teased, curled and feathered by
Allen Edwards of Santa Monica, California.

Sweeping over her eyes and softly framing
the face, her hair created a wonderfully
free-flowing silhouette. At a time when women
wore their hair stiff with hairspray and rigid
with pins, Farrah's was a breath of fresh air,
femininity and freedom.

Posing in a red one-piece swimsuit for one
of the best-selling posters of all time, Farrah
inspired millions of women and seduced teenagers
all over the world. The Farrah flip is forever.

OPPOSITE
Farrah Fawcett.
Hair by Allen Edwards.
Photo Bruce McBroom
1976

FOLLOWING PAGES
Jesus Is My Homeboy.
Photo David LaChapelle
2003

FIRE

'The theme of the calendar was fire, water, ice. For this picture Avedon wanted fire. I had this huge wig prepared at a workshop in Paris. It weighed 5 kilos and we needed five fans to blow the hair. We cut and coloured the hair beforehand. Nadja was really brave – she had to put up with the weight of the wig but also the breeze and the strands of hair whipping her face. She even cried a little. But the result is sublime!

'Working with Avedon was an extraordinary experience. He had an exceptional eye for everything: light, hair, make-up, clothes. The choice of model mattered very much – it was important to him to have a connection with the person he photographed. And there was no showboating on set with him – the atmosphere was studious.'

Yannick d'Is

OPPOSITE
Nadja Auermann
for the Pirelli Calendar,
1995. Hair by Yannick d'Is.

ABOVE
Hair by Laurent Philippon.
Photo Mark Segal
2008

OPPOSITE
Hair by Laurent Philippon.
Photo Anthony Maule
2011

FOLLOWING PAGES
Veruschka. Hair by
Ara Gallant. Photo
Franco Rubartelli
1966

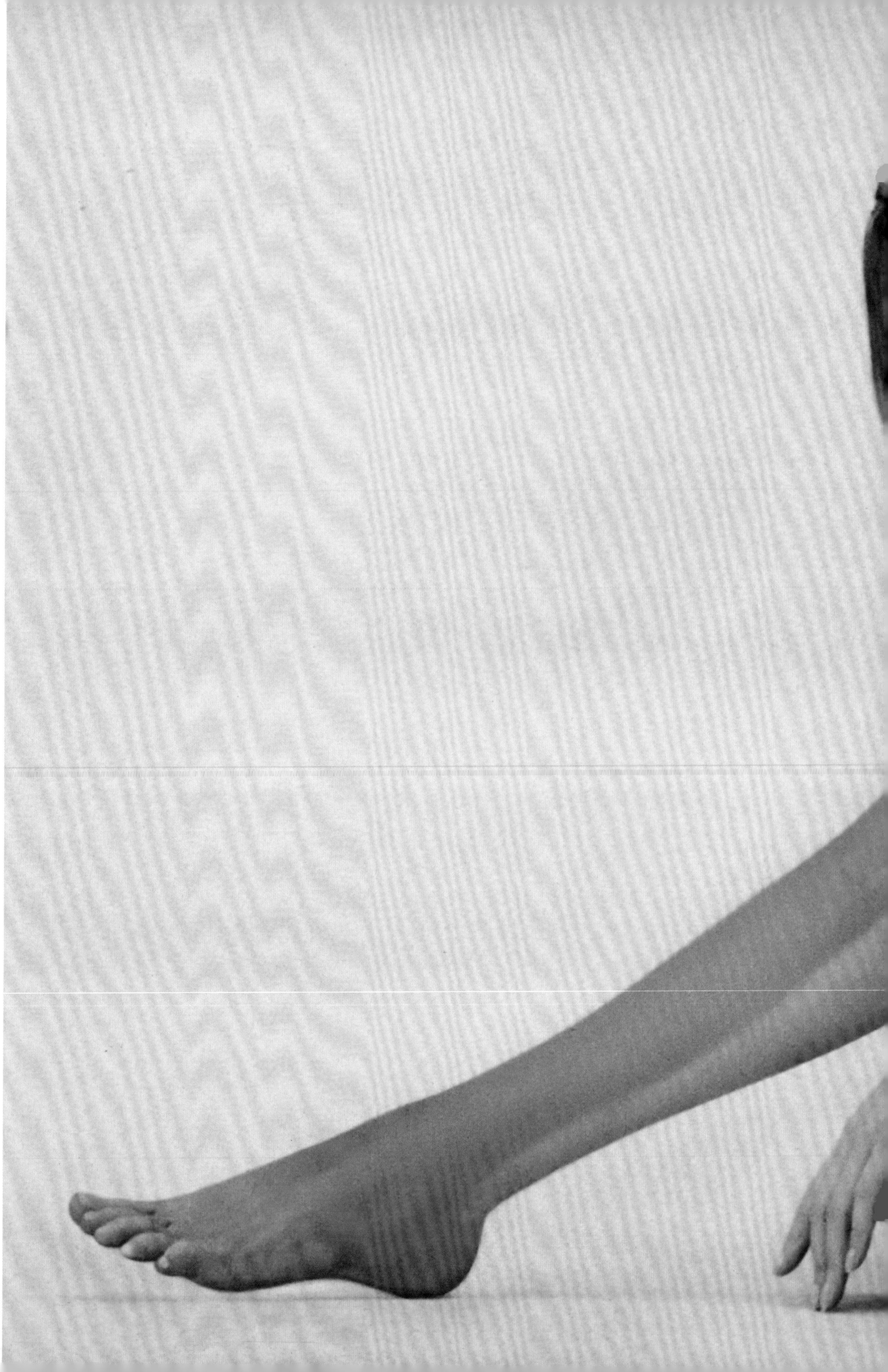

OPPOSITE
Hair by Laurent Philippon.
Photo Sofia Sanchez
and Mauro Mongiello
2008

FOLLOWING PAGES
Photo Patrick Hunt
1973

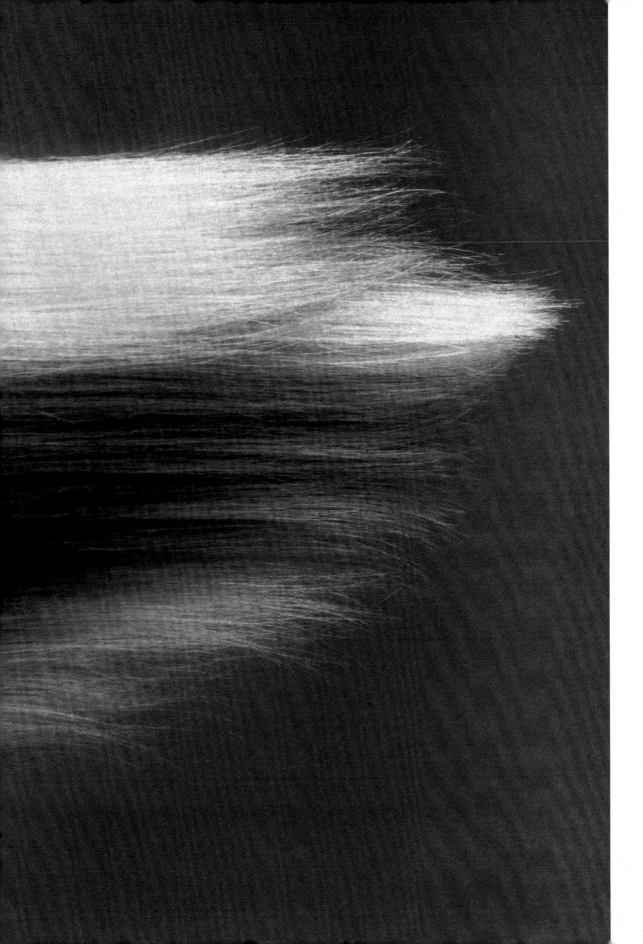

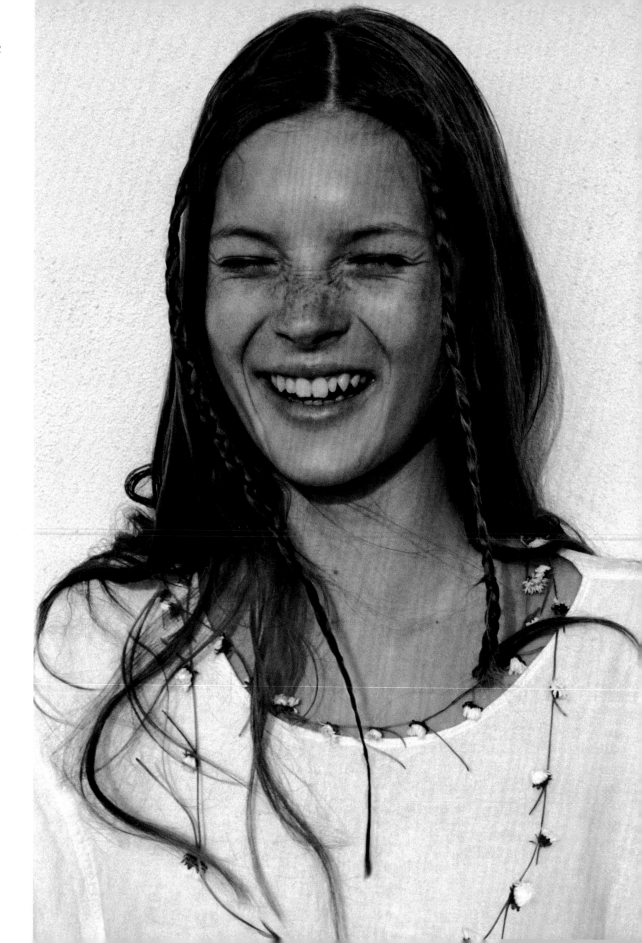

Natasha
Fraser-Cavassoni

KATE MOSS'S
FIRST PHOTO SHOOT

OPPOSITE
Kate Moss. Hair
by Drew Jarrett.
Photo Corinne Day
1990

British-born stylist Melanie Ward has become an acknowledged legend in the fashion industry. She is noted for igniting the revolutionary 'Grunge' movement and being designer Helmut Lang's accomplice and muse for thirteen years. In 1990, with the photographer Corinne Day and a skinny, unknown ingénue called Kate Moss, Ward had little idea that their shoot would change the terms of fashion hairstyling. 'With Kate, we wanted to create something that felt effortless and free,' she says. 'And letting her hair loose like that caught our mood.'

Titled 'The 3rd Summer of Love', and published as the cover story of *The Face* magazine's July issue, the eight pages included clothes by Romeo Gigli and Ralph Lauren. However, it grabbed the industry's attention by showing the teenage, semi-nude Moss laughing, exposing funny pointed teeth and conjuring up playful and waif-like images, particularly when wearing a feather head-dress. 'In that shoot, we were keen to capture the polar opposite of what was going on in other magazines which was polished, perfect and, to our mind, required a bottle of hairspray per look,' says Ward. 'We just felt that was so maximalist whereas our idea of beauty was stripping all that back and showing anti-

perfection.' Like the late Corinne Day, who annoyed Moss's agency for refusing to retouch her photographs and dismissed controlled glossy magazine shoots as being 'stale, just about sex and glamour,' Ward was and continues to encourage an appealing grittiness. 'I just find imperfection much more sexy and beautiful actually,' she says. During the fabled shoot, which took place on a freezing cold day on the beach at Camber Sands in East Sussex, Ward recalls the hairdresser 'running his hand through Kate's hair', which really symbolized their 'thoughts and vision of beauty'. 'Models' appearances were being so pushed and manipulated at the time,' Ward says. 'And we were after something that was young, fresh and cool.'

Afterwards, Day and Ward furthered the aesthetic when they styled ill-kempt youngsters off the street in mismatched vintage clothes. Termed the 'waif look' and bringing to mind Charles Dickens's Artful Dodger and other urchins, it was considered the visual equivalent of Seattle's grunge music and quickly morphed into Grunge. 'What was portrayed in those early photos was very far ahead of how the kids were dressing at the time,' says Ward. 'It was a strong statement about personal style.'

ABOVE
Charlotte Gainsbourg.
Hair by Laurent Philippon.
Photo Serge Leblon
    2004

OPPOSITE
*Joana's back in
the door, Avignon.*
Photo Nan Goldin
    2000

RIGHT
Hair by Laurent Philippon.
Photo David Marvier
2011

ABOVE
Photo Herlinde Koelbl
2007

OPPOSITE
Shirin Neshat – Identified
Photo Cynthia Preston
1995

In Asia and the Middle East hair
is often hidden from public view.
But there are several variations on
an erotic dance style that celebrates
uncovered, free-flying hair.

ARA GALLANT

'Ara Gallant had such wonderful hands
– he could really sculpt hair. He had a real
knowledge of hair and could make it
go in all the directions he wanted and do
unexplainable things.

'It's often forgotten that a great fashion
photograph has to be largely attributed to
the artists behind the camera – the editor,
the stylist, the make-up artist and the hair
stylist. These are the creative forces who
often remain in the shadows.'
Veruschka

RIGHT
Veruschka. Photo
Franco Rubartelli
1968

OPPOSITE
Hair by Laurent Philippon.
Photo Cédric Buchet
2009

Claudine Roméo

A PHILOSOPHY OF HAIR

OPPOSITE
Lakshmi Menon.
Hair by Laurent
Philippon.
Photo Prabuddha
Dasgupta
2010

The first question is: if you can compare the hairdresser with a sculptor, what do you call his medium? In English we talk about 'hair' in the singular, meaning a unified material managed and handled in one collective mass. In Italian 'pasta' is singular as well, although, like hair, it can consist of an almost infinite number of strands. And 'pasta' recalls the original material it comes from, 'paste', from which all the subtle grades of filament can be made. So what is this material, singular and compact, from which an almost infinite number of shapes can be carved? How can the hairdresser be a sculptor, when the material isn't ready to work like a lump of clay? Hair occurs in a fragmented, virtual form, existing as a thousand filaments from the very beginning, fluid, the opposite of compact.

The hairstylist – more than the sculptor – has to model the primary material, to reconstitute it as a single mass, both compact and loose at the same time. You shake your head and if you have long hair it moves like a thick wave. An immaculate square-cut black fringe, worn like a helmet, makes one think of Louise Brooks – in her case the mass of hair moves like a heavy curtain. Draperies in classical sculpture are like this: movement pacified.

A gust of wind, or the stroke of a brush, and suddenly the hair is a scattered mass of strands, like a shower of sparks as they catch the light, a thousand tiny branches.

Hair's multiple character – its particularity – lets it be tied in a ribbon, plaited, curled, straightened, kinked, rolled, or fluffed up, or decorated, just as fine clothes or embroidery: hair can be handled as minutely as a goldsmith's filigree.

But hair can also take on the thickness and mass of clay moulded in bas relief, sitting proud as the hair from the head itself.

In fact, hair can actually evoke clay, ploughed into furrows, regular, shallow or deep. Woven or braided tightly to the surface of the skull, it becomes like short tundra; a collection of plaits can resemble olive or vine groves seen from the air.

But the surface of hair can ripple with tiny waves; or foam, which can be coloured burnt sienna, auburn, russet – more earth terms – a whole geography with roads, streams, waves with wild and pearly reflections. Above all, one sees it in relief: mountains and valleys, stretches of forest and fields, rivers that gleam like sequins.

But there are also the veins of a leaf, the roughness of a tree trunk. In sculpture hair calls to mind something organic, something vegetal. The sculptor strokes the curves of the landscape of the body; the hairdresser works directly on it. And stroking the hair, as one might stroke the fur of a cat, produces magic with his comb. This proximity to the two orders, both animal and vegetable, brings him shoulder to shoulder with the sculptor.

OPPOSITE
Kristen McMenamy.
Photo Philip Riches
2010

COMB CUSTOMS

'The Japanese *kushi* (comb) bears many superstitious meanings: *kushi* is a word associated with sorrow and death, so to lose or break a comb is very bad luck. For the same reason, it is even worse to pick up a lost comb.

'However, a new comb has the power to ward off evil and protect the traveller, symbolically untangling troubles.

'According to an ancient custom, a woman seeking divorce would throw a comb at the feet of her husband.'

Tereza Le Fellic, curator at the Musée du peigne (comb museum), Oyonnax, France

LEFT
Recluse
Photo Alex Stoddard
2012

OPPOSITE
Hair by Laurent Philippon.
Photo Mark Segal
2008

B
L
O
N
D
S

ETC.

1.

2.

3.

4.

1.
Sandro Botticelli, *Birth of Venus*, 1482–1485

2.
Cesare Vecellio, *Venetian lady bleaching her hair*, c. 1590

3.
Nicholas Hilliard, *Margaret of France* (Marguerite de Valois, also known as Queen Margot), 1577. The Queen would often decorate her curls with jewels, or even with golden ringlets cut from the heads of her pageboys.

4.
From *Dangerous Liaisons*, 1988. Wig by Peter Owen. The cone is to protect the face when powdering a wig.

5.
Isabella Rossellini in *Wild at Heart*, directed by David Lynch, 1990. Hair by Frida Aradottir

5.

BLONDS ETC.

It's human nature to want what you don't have. Those with curly hair want it to be straight, those with pale skin want to be dark, the dark long to be fair, those who have blue eyes want brown.

It's not only women. It was British painter David Hockney who said 'Blonds Have More Fun' as he dyed his hair platinum and left grey Great Britain for a sunny life in Los Angeles, the city of Angels, a place that in the 1970s could conceivably have been called the blond capital of the world.

No wonder then, that thousands of years previously olive-skinned, dark-haired Egyptians, Greeks and Persians wanted the fair hair they associated with their gods and goddesses, mythical creatures with hair the colour of the sun and gold, an element they considered to be the 'skin of the gods'.

There are paintings of blonds in Roman civilizations as far back as 750 BC (more than two thousand years before America was discovered, let alone the Californian blond), before we knew the theory that at some point in the distant future, thanks to world migration and intermarriage, the blond Scandinavian gene will die out completely.

Even in Roman times 'blond' had rarity value. As legionaries pillaged the northern Nordic tribes, they cut off the flaxen braids of the vanquished and wore them as trophies.

It was only a matter of time before early Venetian and Roman fashion victims would try to get the look for themselves. In the 15th century going blond involved drastic measures. Women bared their head in the hottest sun, having first coated the hair with a disgusting cocktail of ingredients. Recipes might include sulphur, quicklime, wood ash and saltpetre as well as walnut flowers, elderberries, lupin, myrrh, the dregs of white grapes, madder root and honey; the mixture would be left on for days until a reddish-gold shade evolved, despite the side effects of sunstroke, burned scalps and scarring (not to mention the smell). Quite surprising, then, that it took another three hundred years or so to invent peroxide.

PREVIOUS PAGES
It's My Life. Gwen Stefani.
Hair by Laurent Philippon.
Photo David LaChapelle
2003

Women have always suffered for beauty and 'blond' was associated with beauty even then, as well as with gods and goddesses, angels and therefore goodness and purity. The Virgin Mary was often portrayed as blond, even in dark-haired Europe – think of Botticelli's *Venus*, the original blond bombshell, emerging from the sea.

In fairytales the good and innocent heroine had golden hair, while her potential nemesis was the evil dark-haired witch. From a very early time, blond hair became a symbol of youth and purity as well as a good-luck charm. The blond heroine certainly had more fun, got the Prince and was guaranteed a happy ending.

Assured that there's hardly a downside to life as a blond, it's no wonder that the blond psychology developed. Hair colour is the root of a girl's personality, according to psychologist Dr Tony Fallone in a research paper in 1997. Blond equals innocent, fragile, youthful, cool, chaste and ultimately sexy, kittenish and irresistible – not a colour, then, but a state of mind. Today, thanks to ever more sophisticated ways of colouring hair, it's a lifestyle we can choose at will.

In 1930s Hollywood, it was blonds who saved the box office, from Jean Harlow, Jayne Mansfield, Veronica Lake to Carol Lombard, Marlene Dietrich and Joan Crawford. In the 1950s it was the unforgettable Marilyn. Film-maker Alfred Hitchcock was obsessed with blonds, Grace Kelly being his ultimate ice queen, along with Tippi Hedren and Kim Novak. In the 1960s a new kind of blond evolved: an athletic, gym-toned incarnation, as seen in Cubby Broccoli's Bond films. And while James Bond partied with blonds in Caribbean locations (Ursula Andress, and later Britt Ekland or Kim Basinger, for instance), a new sex kitten, Brigitte Bardot, turned heads on the beach in St Tropez.

In the 1960s directors gave us luminous blond stars like Catherine Deneuve and Anita Ekberg, Julie Christie and Candice Bergen, as well as rock chicks Marianne Faithfull, Patti Boyd and Anita Pallenberg and the German supermodel Veruschka.

The 1970s were a Californian blond moment, with Jane Fonda, Bo Derek (the perfect '10') and finally Farrah Fawcett coming top of a hot list of blonds who men lusted after and women wanted to look like. But with Farrah what we particularly wanted was her hair, a multi-layered, highlighted mane which could be said ultimately to have become the most popular hairstyle in the world.

It's not a huge leap from the Romans and their goddesses to
the modern world worshipping their film, TV, rock and fashion stars
of the moment. The appeal of the blond has spread through hair salons
and across celluloid and now computer screens worldwide. With the
ubiquity of do-it-yourself bleaching the blond has inevitably become
commonplace, not the natural rarity she once was. Today she's
a Baywatch bimbo, a weather girl or a reality-show contestant, rather
than a mysterious and sensuous icon on a pedestal. In fact, she's you
and me and every woman or man. Even those with dark-haired genes
(think Beyoncé, Rihanna and Emeli Sandé) can go blond with patience
and care, thanks to the latest cosmetic science. Now that we have
hair extensions, conditioners, real-hair wigs, talented hairdressers and
colourists, we can all have hair like Farrah or Meg, Madonna, Uma,
Gwyneth, Scarlett, Charlize, Blondie and Kylie; like top models Jerry,
Kate, Claudia, Nadia, Lily, Gisele; like designers Donatella and Jil,
politicians Thatcher or Clinton, TV icons January Jones (*Mad Men*)
or Sarah Jessica Parker (*Sex and the City*).

We can have hair in shades of vanilla, strawberry, ash, gold, butter
or ivory, streaked or painted on, highlighted or low-lighted, discreetly
placed in feathered tips to suggest a recent summer holiday, or all-out
brash peroxide with dark roots showing. We can be blond for a day,
an hour or a week and many say it can even change our lives. Do blonds
still have more fun? Anyone can be the judge of that.

Kathy Phillips

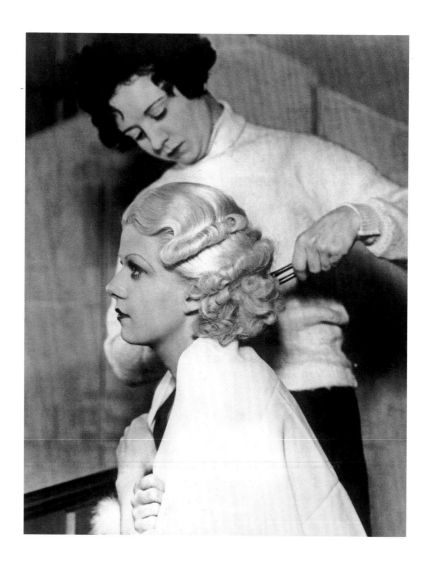

ABOVE
Jean Harlow
1933

OPPOSITE
Hollywood Killer Wave.
Drawing by
Stefano Canulli
2013

VIRNA LISI
Italian actress Virna Lisi (born Virna Pieralisi)
transformed her look many times with
a whole array of hair colours and styles.
She was often typecast as a seductress, but
her role as Catherine de Medici in *La Reine
Margot* (1994) won her the recognition she
deserved, with Cannes and César film awards.
   Clockwise from top: Virna Lisi
in 1963, 1965, 1960, 1964 and (OPPOSITE) 1963.

ABOVE
Meghan Douglas.
Hair by Laurent
Philippon. Photo
Mario Testino
1995

OPPOSITE
*Palm Springs,
California*. Photo
Robert Doisneau
1960

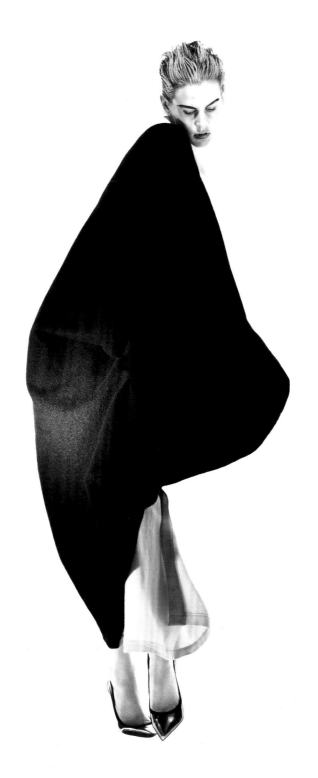

ABOVE
Saskia de Brauw.
Hair by Laurent Philippon.
Photo Jan Welters
2012

OPPOSITE
Claudia Schiffer.
Hair by Laurent Philippon.
Photo Marc Hispard
1995

OPPOSITE
Aline Weber. Hair by
Laurent Philippon.
Photo Paola Kudacki
2008

FOLLOWING PAGES
Daphne Guinness.
Wig by Laurent Philippon,
hair by Tyler Johnston.
Photo Bryan Adams
2010

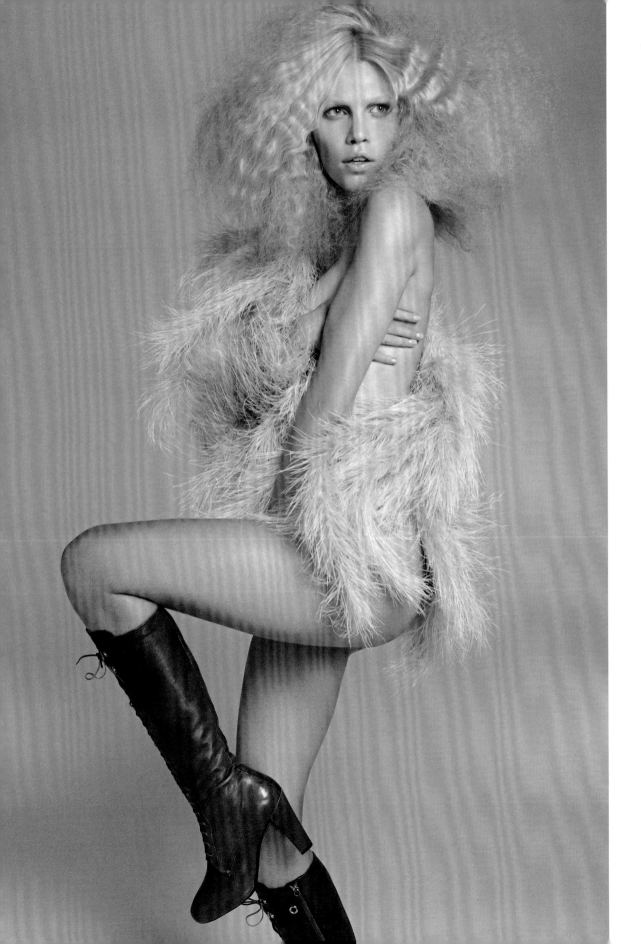

OPPOSITE
Idols. Hair by Peter Savic.
Photo Herb Ritts
1999

Daphne Guinness   *IN BLACK AND WHITE*

OPPOSITE
Daphne Guinness.
Hair by Peter Gray.
Photo François Nars
2009

I used to be taken by my mother to a hairdresser's called Galatea, near Biba, the famous Kensington fashion store of the 1960s and '70s. I was white-blond naturally until I was about eleven years old. Then my hair got a bit darker underneath but stayed light-blond on top.

I started experimenting in my teens, of course. I remember putting a whole bottle of neat hydrogen peroxide all over my hair when I was at college – all my hair turned orange. That wasn't a good idea.

I'm lucky, I have a strong hairline. If I have my hair down everyone says I look younger, but I much prefer it up, and back – civilized.

My mother's hair was very fine, and she never put it up. She was naturally elegant, not in the least eccentric. My father is a thinker – he always has his head in the clouds – but I think I have more his hair than my mother's. My grandmother always wore her hair in a chignon. Perhaps that had a subliminal influence on my style.

My New York hairdresser gave me a Jean Seberg wig for Christmas – it's short, like Audrey Hepburn's hair, or Twiggy's, but black and white. People sometimes claim that hair colour makes a statement – 'blonds are more angelic, brunettes are tougher' – but I think everybody has a soft side and a darker side.

I often dye my hair myself. When I got married, I had blond streaks on top and darker hair underneath. Later, I had a red streak with dark purple underneath, and then it slowly became what it is.

Do I think I'll keep this colour forever? Well, it seems to work… I certainly don't want to spend the rest of my life staring in the mirror.

Hair shows something of a history, a culture and yes, it can be political. It's part of civilization.

OPPOSITE
The Twins. Hair by
Laurent Philippon.
Photo Sebastian Kim
2011

ABOVE
Cyndi Lauper.
Photo Gary Lewis
1984

OPPOSITE
Raquel Zimmermann.
Hair by Laurent Philippon.
Photo Karl Lagerfeld
2008

148

KARL LAGERFELD

Master couturier and style legend Karl Lagerfeld
has worn his hair in a ponytail since 1976, and
it has become a defining part of his look. His hair
is naturally grey, but he prefers to wear it white.

Lagerfeld follows a strict daily dry shampoo
routine – he says: 'I am a walking meringue'.

In the 18th century, according to Lagerfeld,
'no one was young, no one was old. Everyone had
white hair' (*Vogue*, September 2004).

OPPOSITE
Self-portrait.
Photo Karl Lagerfeld
2012

Laurent Philippon   *RED HAIR*

OPPOSITE
Tilda Swinton.
Hair by Sam McKnight.
Photo Craig McDean
2003

Red hair has always been the subject of legends and myths. Believed to be Celtic in origin, red hair has also appeared in ancient Egypt, Greece, northern India, northern Africa and Polynesia.

Recent research suggests that some Neanderthals may have had red hair. A variant of the gene that produces red hair in modern humans provides a tantalizing link to prehistory.

Superstitions and fantasies related to redheads have become anchored in the Western imagination. Being always in the minority, redheads have often been vulnerable to arbitrary attacks. The redhead has been portrayed as malevolent, ominous, deceitful, violent, bloody, sulphurous, erotic and evil, a threat to the moral order.

In 1254 St Louis King of France ordained that prostitutes should dye their hair red to distinguish them from respectable women. Redheads had already become objects of the erotic imagination. In the Middle Ages, however, they were even burned at the stake as witches, red hair being taken for a sign of congress with the devil.

In the 19th century, evolving through representations in poetry and painting, red hair gradually became a symbol of rare and natural beauty.

In advertising, film and fashion media today, red-haired people are still given special status, but now they embody a more positive image – strong, passionate, original, sexy.

Amanda Lepore   *GOING BLOND*

OPPOSITE
Amanda Lepore
as Andy Warhol's
Marilyn (left), and
as Andy Warhol's
Liz (right). Hair by
Laurent Philippon.
Photos David
LaChapelle
2003

The first time I went blond I felt great right away. I wanted to copy Jean Harlow. Blond Hollywood movie stars were the incarnation of beauty. As a transsexual I wanted to be the most feminine and the most glamorous possible.

Jayne Mansfield was a role model for me. She had a lot of surgery and her character was very cartoon-like. She was like an exaggerated Marilyn Monroe – the hair, the tiny waist, the big hips, the big breasts, the kind of body that exists very rarely naturally. The more glamorous and artificial I look the happier I am.

I experimented a lot with hair colour, especially when I was modelling for David LaChapelle: red, purple, pink, black... Dark hair on girls is good for a dominatrix. The only woman with dark hair I ever admired was Bettie Page.

When I had red hair I had to wear tons of make-up. It brought out yellow in my skin. The one good thing was I had a lot of success with men – I always thought men preferred blonds but they really like red hair. I was also yellow for a short time, but I got rid of it because it photographed green.

What I love about being blond is that during the daytime I can go shopping and go to the gym and do the white-trash look with no make-up, and in the evening I can look really fabulous and glamorous.

I like to look untouchable. You have to treat me like a lady and be very delicate with me, not mess me up.

FOLLOWING PAGES
Hair by Laurent Philippon.
Photo Luciana Val and
Franco Musso
2007

SHARON

direction and Julie di ys Outh by ilker Kazel

MARCH 2009

Comme de Garçons

A M A M D A

6 March 2005

PREVIOUS PAGES
Pages from Julien d'Ys'
personal notebook
2009

OPPOSITE
Hair by Laurent Philippon.
Photo Jennifer Tzar
2005

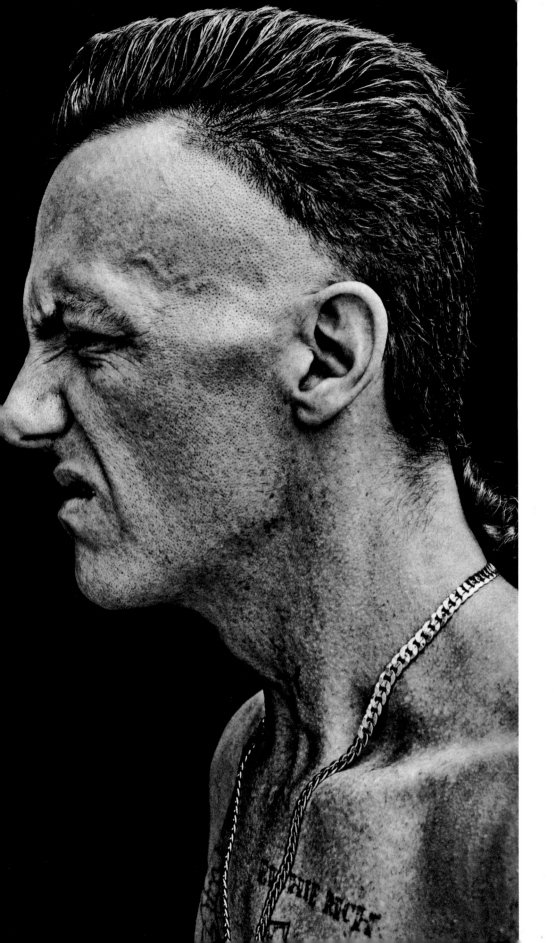

MOHAWKS

1.

2.

3.

1.
Hei Yue, *123 Buttocks*.
Photo Hei Yue,
Beijing 2005

2.
Scody, Crass, Paris.
Photo Ralf Marsault
and Heino Muller, 1988

3.
Roman emperor Hadrian
portrayed as the war
god Mars

THE MOHAWK

THE MOHAWK or Mohican hairstyle gives the human profile a ferocious, animal look. A crest of hair standing up from front to back of the scalp, the Mohawk was long thought to originate with North American tribes, and members of more than one tribe wore the traditional crested hairstyle until the early 20th century.

The Mohawk has often been worn to impress an adversary, to galvanize warriors in battle or to mark social status. As a fashion style it evokes a rebel spirit on the edges of society.

Despite its North American names, however, the crested style has been found in more than one civilization and on more than one continent. Members of some African tribes have always traditionally styled their hair into crests, as shown by ancient artefacts.

There are some ancient European examples too: in Ireland the preserved body of a man, known as Clonycavan Man and dating back 2300 years, was found wearing a Mohawk hairstyle, with traces of an ancient sort of hair gel made from vegetable oils and pine resin.

Helmets from the time of the Roman Empire often bore a long crest worn in a very similar style to the Mohawk, with plumes or horsehair often coloured red and set high, giving the wearer imposing extra height. More recently, in the Second World War, US Special Forces adopted the look, in a powerful expression of esprit de corps.

In London in the 1970s, members of the punk movement famously made the style their own as an outrageously visible sign of breaking with conventional society. They dyed their hair bright day-glo colours, and created a range of wild shapes and spikes using hairspray or even glue to stiffen them.

In the 1990s, the style was made over in a more glamorous mode and was featured on haute couture catwalks and in the glossiest fashion magazines.

PREVIOUS PAGES
Die Antwoord
(Yolandi and Ninja).
Photo Sebastian Kim
2010

1.

2.

3.

1.
Harpocrates, the Greek god adapted from the Egyptian child god Horus. The lock of hair at the side of the figure's head indicates childhood.

2.
Tikar women, Cameroon, 1930s

3.
In the ancient kingdom of Benin, the Yoruba messengers of the king shaved their heads except for a braided tuft in the middle of the skull. They conveyed royal orders to the people and enforced the laws. Their fearsome appearance lent them authority.

OPPOSITE
Tutsi chief with a 'Mutussi' style, Rwanda
1923

2.

1.

3.

4.

1.
Native American
roach made from wild
turkey beard from
the Sac and Fox tribe,
c. 1920

2.
Native American
Klickitat Brave. Photo
Benjamin A. Gifford,
1899

3.
Bear Bull, Blackfoot,
Alberta. Photo
Edward S. Curtis,
1926

4.
Plenty Coups, chief
of the Crow. Photo
Edward S. Curtis,
1908

MOHAWK AND MOHICAN

The Mohawk tribe of America has given its name to the hairstyle. However, there were other tribes among the Iroquois of northeastern America who wore similar styles, such as the Mohicans (the word by which the style has become known in Britain). It was also worn symbolically in the form of a roach, an artificial crest made from animal hair and skin.

Photographs taken by Edward Curtis opened people's eyes to the North American Indian. But according to Josephine Paterek, author of the *Encyclopedia of American Indian Costume*, American Indians only began to learn about their history in the 20th century. Cowboy films, Westerns, showed an over-simplified Hollywood image of the tribes wearing elaborate hair and feather crests. Thanks to television the Mohawk spread across America and the world.

RIGHT
American parachutists,
with their hair cut
Mohawk-style for good
luck and 'esprit de corps',
prepare for their mission.
Arras, France, 23 March
1945. Photo Robert Capa

*Natasha
Fraser-Cavassoni*

LONDON'S PUNK SCENE

OPPOSITE
A group of punks
facing eviction from
the house they were
squatting, King's
Cross, London
1979

Punk Rock aimed to create pandemonium. Adopted by the young, old, poor and privileged, the cultural phenomenon swept through Thatcher's Britain during the mid-'70s. Bristling with rage, it rebelled against the class system, grim living situations, unemployment and other social injustices.

Whatever the Punk Rocker's look – whether it involved major eye make-up, facial piercing, ripped T-shirts pieced together with safety pins and bondage trousers – 'the filth and the fury', as termed by the *Daily Mirror* newspaper, began with the hair. Often dyed, it ranged from being hedgehog-like – short, spiky and greased – to boasting fabulously tall Mohawk styles (known in Britain as Mohicans) whose height was further emphasized by the owner's shaved scalp.

The King's Road in Chelsea had the most exaggerated examples. No doubt because it had become a Punk Rock mecca. This was thanks to Seditionaries, previously known as SEX, the boutique run by Malcolm McLaren and his then girlfriend Vivienne Westwood. Seditionaries sold the best of Punk regalia but, most importantly, was a direct link to the Sex Pistols, the Punk band that was managed by McLaren.

Since Punk Rock's genesis was the music world, there were many key bands such as the Ramones, the Dead Kennedys and the Clash, but few captured Great Britain's imagination like the Pistols. Their bestselling single 'God Save the Queen' – released during Elizabeth II's Silver Jubilee year – 'gobbed' gloriously in the face of the establishment. Not only because of its outrageous lyrics and defaced poster of the British monarch but also due to the easily imitated haircuts of band members Johnny Rotten and Sid Vicious.

As Seditionaries was situated at World's End, far away from the Tube, the punks – who travelled in packs – had to march the entire length of the King's Road. Watching them in progress was equivalent to being faced with an aviary of scowling birds of prey. Eyes were encircled by kohl black, chains ran from their nose to their ear, while their hairstyles screamed attitude. A group of female punks would be standing together sporting dos that were either peroxide yellow, bright pink or apple, while their male equivalent might look severe with pale faces and blue-black spikes.

But perhaps the most magnificent were the Mohicans. Some were bright, others were dark, the tips of the spikes dyed with a rainbow-array of colours. Yet ultimately it was the defiant expression on their faces that questioned why people were staring, as if to assert: this is perfectly normal. It typified British nonchalance.

RIGHT
Punks on the King's Road,
Chelsea, London, 1970s.
Photo Ted Polhemus

LEFT
Alice Dellal.
Photo Adrian Wilson
2009

RIGHT
Photo Carl W. Heindl
2009

OPPOSITE
Actor, performer and
legendary drag artist
Divine as Babs Johnson
in *Pink Flamingos*,
directed by John Waters,
1972. Hair by David
Lochary and Mink Stole

RIGHT
A mother and daughter,
Newport, Wales.
Photo Martin Parr
1988

RIGHT
Isabelle Adjani in
Subway, directed by
Luc Besson. Hair by
Isabelle Gamsohn
1985

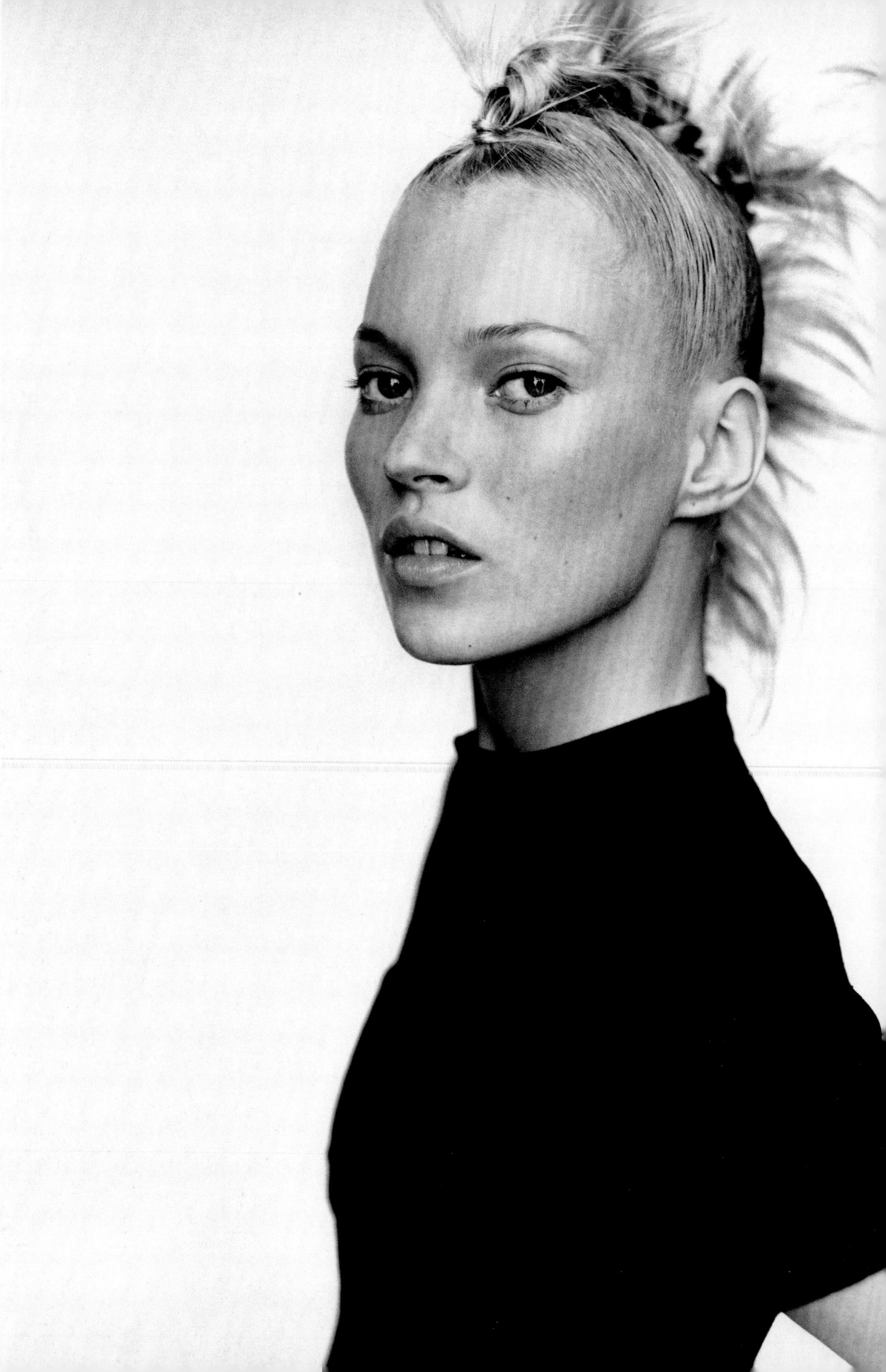

Orlando Pita

THE GLAMOROUS MOHAWK

OPPOSITE
Kate Moss. Hair
by Orlando Pita.
Photo Mario Testino
1996

My mother would go to the hairdresser once a week and get this really tall beehive. The first time I was shocked. I thought: 'But where's my mother?' She would wrap it in a silk scarf at night and in the morning, she would take a rat-tail comb and pump it up.

At 14 my brother and I decided that he'd cut my hair and I'd cut his – it couldn't be worse than the hairdresser. I cut his first and it was really bad, so I didn't let him cut mine. That was the end of the deal. But I started to wonder what I did wrong. I asked my grandmother if I could cut her hair, and she let me. Then I did hair for my school friends, and anyone else I could convince.

When I was 21, my brother was working for a fashion photographer, and the hairdresser cancelled so they called me. The photographer's agent said: 'I think you have something and I'd like to represent you.'

I thought, let's try it and see – I don't need a licence. Nine months later I moved to Paris and started working there.

In the beginning I was into getting everything perfect and sculptural. Then I wanted to destroy that perfection – I started to get into the fuzzy texture, casual hair, easy-going hair. I loved the street looks in New York in the '70s and '80s. A friend of mine was a colourist at Bumble and bumble, and Michael Gordon saw my work and liked it. That's how we started to work together.

I always loved the way Ara Gallant did hair for Richard Avedon's photographs. I was inspired without knowing who he was. I wasn't working with the classic hairdressing tools, I would do whatever it took. I would sculpt more, I would build, rather than using curling irons or rollers. Being technical came later.

I got a taste for fashion. I knew how to sew – I used it quite often to build up hairstyles – and for a while I thought I could become a designer but I realized they work all the time, they don't go home like I do.

Kate's hairstyle for the cover of *The Face* is inspired by the Mohawk, but it's not a Mohawk. It's aggressive but flattering. I don't like ugly, I like beauty – if I do a style a bit rock 'n' roll it has to be glamorous too. I like the macabre and the dark, but I have to make it beautiful.

When punks started to come to St Mark's Place in New York wearing Mohawks in the early '80s, it was a movement that came with a look. Now the kids do it as fashion. That's how I reinterpreted it with Kate. Trends used to be related to a social movement. Nowadays there are no big political movements that have a meaning, there's nothing to fight for.

When I did the beehive for Prada everyone said the beehive is trendy. I was like 'Really? I haven't seen anyone wearing a beehive…' Trend forecasting is for sponsors.

ABOVE
Maggie Rizer.
Hair by Laurent Philippon.
Photo Ben Hassett
2007

OPPOSITE
Hair by Laurent Philippon.
Photo Anthony Maule
2011

SAM MCKNIGHT

'I was 18 years old, studying in college to
be a teacher, and hating it. My friend owned
a nightclub, a restaurant and a hairdressing salon
all in the same building, right there where I lived
in a small town by the sea in Scotland. I started
to help in the salon and loved it right away.

'In the summer of 1975 I went to London and
got completely hooked. Everything was changing:
platform shoes, crazy colour in the hair... David
Bowie ruled. Then Malcolm McLaren and Vivienne
Westwood opened the shop SEX on the King's
Road and the punk movement started.

'Later I worked at Molton Brown where I met
and worked with Kerry Warn. I was also doing
a lot of romantic styles, which I still love to do,
with soft braids and silk tied in the hair.

'I met Diana Princess of Wales on a shoot for
British *Vogue* with Patrick Demarchelier in 1990.
She wanted to change her hairstyle, so I cut
it very short and slicked back – she loved it.
I went on to travel with her for seven years.'
Sam McKnight

LEFT
Hair by Sam McKnight.
Photo Paolo Roversi
2010

RIGHT
Hair by Laurent Philippon.
Photo David Marvier
2011

LEFT
Hair by Laurent Philippon.
Photo Joe Lally
2006

ABOVE
Mohican, London.
Photo Martin Parr
1997

OPPOSITE
Hair by Laurent Philippon.
Photo Sofia Sanchez
and Mauro Mongiello
2009

OPPOSITE
Hair by Orlando Pita.
Photo Craig McDean
2004

C H I G N O N S

1.

2.

3.

1.
Marie de' Medici, second wife of Henri IV of France, in 1601. Marie's distinctive chignon was different from the style of his first wife (see Margaret, p. 124) whose 'à bouffon' style had been the height of court fashion.

2.
Pisanello, detail from *St George and the Princess of Trebizond*, c. 1438. The Princess was a legendary beauty, said to have married her father's enemy out of political necessity.

Her voluminous chignon is held by a 'basket' of crossed bands of gold and silk thread. Long hair was considered an erotic feminine attribute that had to be carefully controlled.

3.
Portrait of an aristocratic Roman woman during the Flavian dynasty (AD 69–96). Curls are piled high at the front; the hair is braided and coiled into a chignon at the back.

THE CHIGNON is a way of drawing the hair up, revealing the back of the neck.

The simplest form of chignon is the ponytail; the most complex chignons are intricate wonders that show off the hairdresser's ingenuity and give the wearer a sense of enormous wellbeing.

Hair is the most natural and adaptable kind of ornamentation. It can be endlessly shaped and sculpted into surprising new forms. The chignon can be decorated with jewels or flowers and can support all kinds of diadems, tiaras and crowns.

Until very recently, in many cultures women did not appear in public with their hair down. Asian women, blessed with hair that can grow wonderfully long, excel in the art of the chignon. The sophistication of different styles belongs to a great tradition of Asian decorative arts going back thousands of years.

In 5th-century Rome hairstyle played an important role in the art of self-presentation. Roman women, known for their flirtatious ways, competed with each other to create ever more ingenious and sophisticated chignons to attract male attention.

In the 15th century Theodora Commene, Princess of Trebizond, wore a famously extravagant chignon. In a society obsessed with luxury and jewels, size and ostentation showed off the wearer's status.

In the 20th century Alexandre de Paris was often called 'the king of the chignon'. He styled some of the most important crowned heads in the world, as well as the catwalk models of the greatest Parisian couturiers of the time, such as Dior, Chanel and Yves Saint Laurent.

In the 1960s creative hairstyling burst into life after the austerity of the war years. More voluminous than ever, chignons from this era continue to influence styles today, especially those associated with the popular stars of music and film.

PREVIOUS PAGES
Sarah Thom. Photo
Jerry Schatzberg
1962

ALEXANDRE DE PARIS
Alexandre Raimon learned his trade at
the salon of the great Antoine de Paris.

In 1952 he opened his own salon in Paris
on the Faubourg Saint Honoré and quickly
became a fashion celebrity in his own right
– naturally known as Alexandre de Paris.

Alexandre's friend, the artist Jean Cocteau,
encouraged Alexandre to make sketches of
his creations. Alexandre's signed drawings, with
their ornate chignons, plaits, pompons, silk
ribbons and gems, became keenly sought after.

Ligne
Hispano

Printemps
Été
1974

Alexandre
74

*Natasha
Fraser-Cavassoni*

ALEXANDRE DE PARIS

OPPOSITE
Alexandre de Paris.
Photo Ronald Traeger
1967

Parisian chic and Monsieur Alexandre de Paris went hand-in-hand. In his heyday, which continued until the mid-1990s, he worked for all the great designers like Coco Chanel, Yves Saint Laurent, Hubert de Givenchy, Karl Lagerfeld, Jean-Paul Gaultier and Thierry Mugler. He also snipped the tresses of Elizabeth Taylor, Greta Garbo, Audrey Hepburn, Sophia Loren, Maria Callas and Grace of Monaco, and dreamt up the impeccable dos at Marie-Hélène de Rothschild's Proust Ball and other memorable events.

Few hairdressers are capable of seamlessly mixing fashion with society but Monsieur Alexandre became a relied-upon power in both worlds. His gifts included being a superb technician – at a glance, he recognized how a face should be framed – and being stimulated by the new. General-like, he approached each fashion season with a flourish and was prudently tight-lipped, aware that careless talk lost clients.

Monsieur Alexandre was too much of a sly fox to become arrogant but he knew his worth and realized his instincts were golden. Shaping Elizabeth Taylor's long mane into his iconic artichoke crop illustrated this. Famously, she burst into tears, and then realized that the new style drew attention to her violet eyes,

exquisite profile and suited her femme fatale existence.

When preparing Jacqueline de Ribes for an American fashion shoot, he drove her mad with his intricate plaiting, but the hairdresser understood the business of legends and was merely strengthening her reputation as a Paris-based style icon.

Short in stature with a little pencil moustache, his immaculate yet slightly dated attire of double-breasted jacket and belted pants brought to mind a French character actor from the 1970s with elements of Hercule Poirot. His salon's insignia was a phoenix, sketched by the artist Jean Cocteau, the hairdresser's pal, and behind the gilded and glass doors of the avenue Matignon establishment, Marie-Hélène de Rothschild and others would wait their turn.

Monsieur Alexandre's team became renowned for their chignons. Going there at the age of 18 became a rite of passage for certain aristocratic Parisians. And when he sold off the salon, which still continues and includes an active hair accessories business, most of Monsieur Alexandre's devotees successfully opened shop and developed their own sparkling clientele.

OPPOSITE
Jean Shrimpton, evening
dress by Galitzine, hair by
Alexandre, August 1965,
Paris studio. Photograph
by Richard Avedon.

OPPOSITE
Homage to *The Shanghai
Gesture*. Hair by
Laurent Philippon.
Photo Ali Mahdavi
2001

RIGHT
Raquel Zimmermann
and Julien d'Ys.
Head stylist Julien d'Ys.
Photo Annie Leibovitz
2008

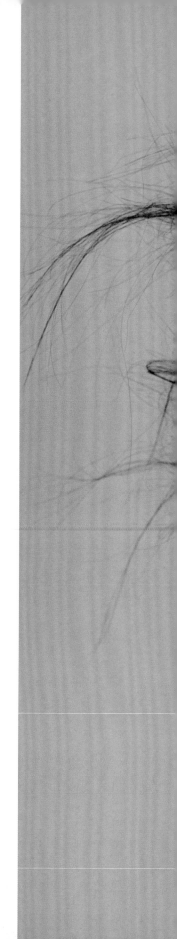

RIGHT
Hair by Laurent Philippon.
Photo David Marvier
2011

LEFT
Lucie de la Falaise.
Hair by Laurent Philippon.
Photo Jeanloup Sieff
1990

216

OPPOSITE
Hair by Laurent Philippon.
Photo Anthony Maule
2010

ABOVE
Natalie Portman
in *Star Wars Episode 1:
The Phantom Menace*,
directed by George Lucas,
1999. Hair by Sue Love

OPPOSITE
Hair by Laurent Philippon.
Photo Alex Cayley
2004

NO LOOKING BACK

Julien d'Ys

I've always loved creating. I dreamed of going to art school, but my father didn't want me to go. I studied architecture without being really motivated.

Then I got an apprenticeship in a hair salon. I ended up working for Jean-Louis David in Paris. At the time he worked closely with Helmut Newton. I started to work regularly in the studio with Peter Lindbergh and Paolo Roversi.

I went to New York in the early '80s and worked with Steven Meisel just at the start of his career. We got on really well: no looking back at what had been done before, just creating from scratch.

I began to deconstruct hairstyles. I would take classics and give them a more tousled, sexy look. I liked to give the impression that the hair had already 'lived' for a few days.

In the early '90s I opened my own agency in Paris, Atlantis, with Yannick, François Leroy and Linda Cantello. We did fashion shows: Comme des Garçons, Yohji Yamamoto, Gucci by Tom Ford, Zucca, Jean Colonna and Chanel for Karl Lagerfeld. We did a lot of shows with John Galliano.

I get the spirit of the shoot and straight away I know what I can bring to the image. I like to get to work as soon as I have an idea, I don't waste time.

Last night I saw a film about Michelangelo. He didn't want to be a painter, he wanted to be a sculptor. But he was recognized as a painter. I'd love to be better known for my painting than for my hair.

OPPOSITE
Julien d'Ys' personal notebook, 2009, with photo of Karlie Kloss by Patrick Demarchelier. Head stylist Julien d'Ys

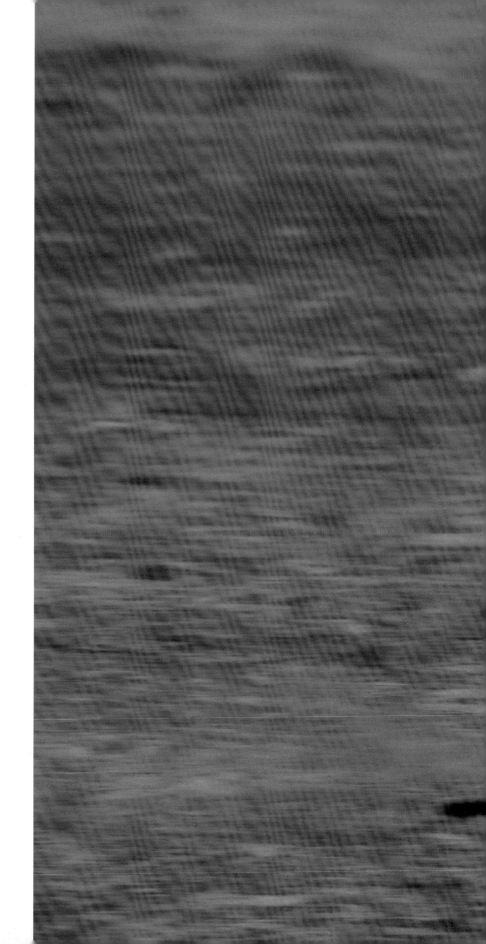

RIGHT
Naomi Campbell.
Hair by Laurent Philippon.
Photo Jean-Paul Goude
2009

WIGS

1.

2.

1.
Ancient stone relief
at the temple of
Kom Ombo, Egypt,
1st century BC

2.
King Seti I and
the goddess Hathor,
from Seti's tomb
in the Valley of Kings,
c. 1280 BC

3.
Still from *Fellini's Casanova*,
directed by Federico
Fellini, 1976. Hair
by Gabriella Borzelli

3.

THE WIG has many uses: to protect against the sun, to hide physical imperfection, to change the look or colour of one's hair, or even to mark social status. In ancient Egypt wigs were worn for all these reasons, the finest on the heads of pharaohs and divinities.

Men and women would shave their heads throughout the Middle East, and would wear a wig for ceremony or show. In the 5th century BC in Athens it was not rare to see wigs being worn by men and women alike. After the conquest of Gaul by Julius Caesar in the 1st century BC it became fashionable for Romans to adopt different wigs to let them change into blonds or redheads, both hair colours being more common in northern Europe. A market quickly grew for Roman women who wished to change their hairstyle as often as three times a day.

Elaborate and expensive wigs indicated the wearer could afford the finest personal decoration. Elizabeth I of England had an impressive collection of wigs, from which she chose according to what she was wearing that day. Louis XIII of France and his son Louis XIV advanced the fashion for wigs among gentlemen and court nobles, guaranteeing long careers for expert wigmakers.

In 17th century France the art of the wig reached its peak. Ladies at the court of Marie Antoinette carried the fashion to its height in the 18th century, extending their own hair into extravagant towering creations, competing crazily for attention.

The 'nihongami' hairstyle was worn by courtesans from the Japanese Edo period (1603–1868) onwards, and is still worn today by geishas for traditional ceremonies, although it is elaborate and requires skilled maintenance; the wearer must sleep with a special neck support. For both reasons wigs are increasingly used instead.

In the West, however, wigs are most commonly noticed on the heads of actors or judges. Fashionable pleasure-seekers may prefer hair extensions; they, too, enjoy the liberation of adopting another identity.

PREVIOUS PAGES
Hair by Laurent Philippon.
Photo Richard Burbridge
2006

1.
In 1779 Paris was seized by the fashion for enormous hairpieces; coaches had to be completely refitted to accommodate the ladies' coiffure.

2.
A portrait of the Queen Marie Antoinette's close friend the Princesse de Lamballe.

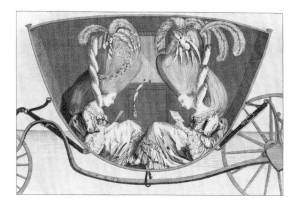

1.

3.

3.
Léonard Autié was Marie Antoinette's personal hairdresser. In her honour he created architectural wonders out of hair decorated with feathers, flowers, pearls and other jewelry. Léonard was responsible for some of the wildest fancies at the Court. He could conjure up a style with a cage containing live butterflies, or the famous 'À la Belle Poule', a coiffure complete with mast and sails, named for a French frigate in 1780.

The fashion for extravagant hair ended with the French Revolution of 1789, when many of his customers (including the Princesse de Lamballe) lost their heads to the guillotine. Léonard survived to write his memoirs.

2.

4.

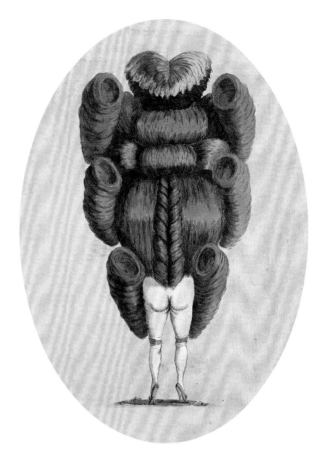

6.

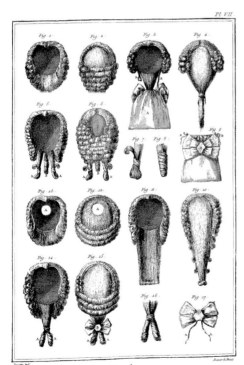

5.

4.
Wig seller, Paris,
1770s.

5.
In the 18th century wigs
were an essential fashion
accessory for men and
women.

6.
Caricature by an
anonymous French artist,
late 18th century. Lady
Laycock was famed for
her elaborate wig that
caught light in a chandelier.
Harper's Magazine
described the kind of
wig as 'an actual tower
of true and false hair,
rags, ribbons, feathers,
powder, and pomatum.'
She even featured
in a poetic warning:

'Yet Miss at her rooms
Must beware of her
          plumes;
For if Vulcan her feather
          embraces,
Like poor Lady Laycock
She'll burn like a
          haycock,
And roast all the loves
          and the graces.'

THE ART OF THE GEISHA

Geishas are women whose traditional role
is to entertain wealthy clients. They must master
poetry, music and dance.

A geisha's appearance follows very strict
aesthetic codes. They wear a kimono and arrange
their hair in a bun in a style called 'shimada'.
Today, so few hairdressers can make a genuine
shimada that the style is commonly worn as
a wig. Developed in the 17th century, the style
has become the emblem of the traditional
Japanese hairstyle. It is composed of several
intricately arranged volumes decorated with
combs and hairpins.

The shape of the shimada differs depending
on the maturity of the wearer. Some find
the curvaceous shapes of the shimada suggest
the curves of the female body.

RIGHT
Photo Horace Bristol
late 1940s / early 1950s

238

1.

2.

3.

1.
Coiffure recreated from
the time of Louis XVI
for Cécile Sorel,
Comtesse de Ségur

2.
Style created for
Josephine Baker

3.
Roman ceremonial
headdress as worn by
Arletty in *Les Joies
du capitole*, 1935

OPPOSITE
Greek hairstyle inspired
by classical art

ANTOINE DE PARIS

Polish-born Antoni Cierplikowski (1884–1976)
created 'haute coiffure', raising a craft to
an art. He arrived in Paris in 1903 at the age of
17, and made his name as Antoine de Paris.

Passionately creative and always in search
of innovative techniques, Antoine developed
a lacquer made with gum arabic for making
incredible sculptural wigs.

In 1938, he presented the great epochs
in the history of hairdressing at a grand dinner at
the Ambassadors' Theatre on the Champs Elysées.

Antoine featured examples of the hairstylist's
art from the empires of Persia, Greece, Rome,
Africa, China, Egypt at the time of Nefertiti,
and Botticelli's Renaissance Italy, as well as an
homage to Marie Antoinette. All the wax heads
shown were made specially for Antoine by Paris's
waxworks museum, the Musée Grévin.

Ewa Ziembinska

OPPOSITE
Hair by James Pecis.
Photo Jason Kibbler
        2012

FOLLOWING PAGES
Daphne Guinness.
Hair by Laurent Philippon.
Photo David LaChapelle
        2002

David LaChapelle   GOOD HAIR, BAD HAIR

OPPOSITE
Love Me. Hair by
Laurent Philippon.
Photo David
LaChapelle
2002

My first hair memory is of breaking my mom's hairdryer, the helmet kind that you put your head under. That would have been in the 1960s. Then in the 1970s she went through a wig moment. When my mom was out I would put on her wig and watch TV.

When I was growing up, all the kids had short hair. But my mom was great – she didn't believe in haircuts, she would let me have long hair down to my shoulders. I felt very glamorous. I loved how it felt when I would ride my bike and my hair would be blowing on my back, it gave me so much pleasure.

When I was about 12 or 13 blond streaks were in fashion, and I shoplifted a blond highlights kit from the drugstore. You were supposed to leave it on for 15 minutes, but that sounded way too subtle for me so I slept in it. In the morning I had these crazy white stripes, so I wore a hat for a whole week. Then I went and shoplifted some hair colour – Clairol ash brown, I'll never forget. It looked great the first day but after I used shampoo it turned green. Along with my green hair I'd also started using new instant tanning cream, which turned my face the colour of a tangerine… it was quite a combination.

I really loved punk rock hairstyles, especially the first really shocking ones. In New York in the early 1980s there was so much variety, a real culture clash. You had all these different urban tribes and they all had a specific style: disco, punk rock, Afro. You'd know everything about a person by looking at the way they wore their hair: you could tell if they lived uptown or downtown, what kind of music they were into, if they did coke or heroin, if they were gay or straight…

Of course I have my likes and dislikes. I love big frizzy wild crimped hair but it doesn't suit everybody. And I love blond hair but it has to have dark roots. For me blond hair symbolizes trashy! The first blond I was in love with was Debbie Harry. When a girl is so confident that she can keep her dark roots with white-blond hair, and the ends are frazzled, I think it's gorgeous.

OPPOSITE
Airbrushed Wings.
Hair by Laurent
Philippon. Photo
David LaChapelle
2002

But there is and there always will be bad hair. It's fake naturalism that I really hate, like hair extensions. I don't like white-girl hair on a black girl – I love the creativity of what black girls do with their hair that you can trace back to Africa, it has a culture.

If you want to be a fashion photographer you have to love make-up and you have to love clothes, and you'd better know the difference between good and bad hair. When I first started out as a photographer I was doing the hair myself, and when I didn't know what to do, I would slick it back because I knew that bad hair could ruin a photograph.

Disasters can happen. In the 1980s I was working for Andy Warhol's *Interview* magazine in New York. I was shooting a Nashville country and western star in my East Village apartment. She was wearing prairie dresses and jeans, but then the stylist dressed her in Steven Sprouse, all day-glo and graffiti-inspired. The hairdresser took all of her super-long hair, pulled it up on top of her head in a ponytail and put rubber bands around it every two inches until it stood straight up on her head, and finally he shaped the top like a palm tree. This poor girl was turned into a new-wave monster. What could I do? I had to take just close-up details instead...

When I hire great people I let them do their thing. Once I did a shoot with Daphne Guinness, and Laurent did her hair like Princess Leia from *Star Wars* – that brought a whole new dimension to the shoot. That's what happens when you work with the best people.

OPPOSITE
Helena Christensen.
Hair by Peter Savic.
Photo Herb Ritts
1996

NAGI NODA: HAIR HATS
Japanese artist Nagi Noda's sculptural 'hair hats' are whimsical animal forms, intricately woven from a combination of the models' own hair and beautifully crafted extensions.

The results combine a childlike sensibility with a surrealistic strangeness. Björk wore one of Nagi Noda's creations for a music tour, and the pieces have been the subject of several exhibitions including at Tokyo's Creation Gallery G8 and Colette, Paris.

An extraordinary and influential talent, Nagi Noda's work in photography and video explored the worlds of fashion and music with fearless originality until her premature death in 2008.

Photos Kenneth Cappello

OPPOSITE
Hair by Laurent Philippon.
Photo Miles Aldridge
2010

RIGHT
Comme des Garçons
couture show
autumn–winter 2012–13.
Head stylist Julien d'Ys.
Photo Ilker Akyol
2012

LEFT
Hair by Laurent Philippon.
Photo Greg Lotus
2006

OPPOSITE
Mariacarla Boscono
and Anja Rubik. Hair
by Laurent Philippon.
Photo Patrick Demarchelier
2008

SHORT
HAIR

2.

1.

1.
Actress Eva Lavallière began the new fashion in France for short hair for women, thanks to famous stylist Antoine de Paris who transformed her look in 1909. By the 1920s the 'bob' was part of the modern woman's new independent identity.

2.
Antoine de Paris, c. 1928

3.
Sisters G., Vienna, c. 1930. Photo Studio Manassé

3.

SHORT HAIR

Usually associated with masculine occupations such as farming, hunting, and other physical activities, short hair for women is considered rare. A shaved female head is even thought of as unnatural, although the style is not new.

In ancient Egypt heads were shaved for hygiene; for the Lobi tribe in West Africa shaved heads are considered beautiful and are observed during rites of passage, marriages, initiations and other socially important ceremonies.

Cutting off hair has often symbolized a removal of individuality, whether imposed on slaves or soldiers, or as a punishment for outcasts, collaborators or convicts. For Buddhist monks, shaving one's head bare expresses humility and willingness to renounce earthly cares. Joan of Arc's cropped head, however, signifies a woman who has given up her outer femininity and shows her inner strength.

In Paris in the 19th century the Titus crop (named after the Roman emperor) became fashionable for both men and women, who wore their hair shockingly short and wig-free. It provoked violent arguments about whether it was ever suitable for a woman to be seen this way. In Japan during the Edo period middle-class women cut their hair to save time and money, but in 1872 the government banned short hair for women, judging it too masculine.

In 1909 Antoine de Paris cut the hair of French actress Eva Lavallière and launched the 20th century's first fashion for short hair for women. By the 1920s this androgynous style was worn by couturier Coco Chanel, crossed the Atlantic and was adopted by Hollywood stars such as Louise Brooks.

Short hair was worn by women more freely in the 1960s, as social rules became more liberated and women went to work. Vidal Sassoon's new short geometrical cut was easy to maintain and suited the active modern woman. At the end of the 1960s skinheads first appeared in London. Although it appears to be the ultimate anti-style, the shaved head carries meaning and symbolism that extends far back in history.

PREVIOUS PAGES
Still from *Who Are You, Polly Maggoo?*, directed by William Klein, 1966.
Hair by Vidal Sassoon

'HAIR BY ANTOINE DE PARIS'
Antoine achieved a remarkable modernity
of shape and proportion, recalling the Art
Deco style, combining fluidity with precision.

Having started the 20th-century fashion
for women's hair cropped short ('à la garçonne'),
he styled the hair of many Hollywood stars.
He counted Sarah Bernhardt among his clients,
he created Josephine Baker's famous curls and
Greta Garbo's pageboy cut.

Antoine's creative skills became legendary.
Success brought him two aeroplanes, a yacht,
and a car specially coachbuilt for him in black
tortoiseshell. He opened dozens of hairdressing
salons in Europe, and more than one hundred in
the United States. In his famous Paris apartment,
he slept on a crystal bed in the shape of a coffin.

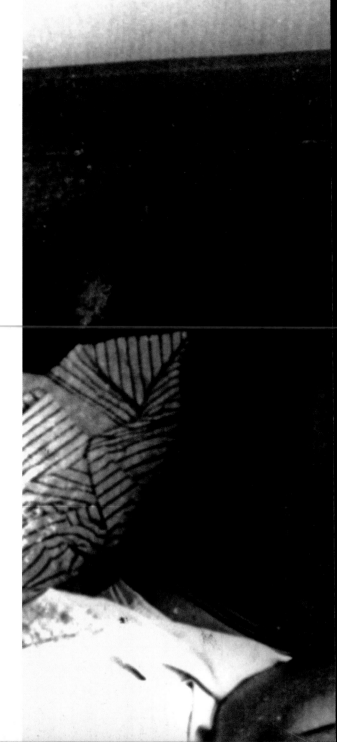

RIGHT
Jean Seberg and Jean-Paul Belmondo, *A bout
de souffle* (Breathless), 1960. Seberg made
her film début three years earlier in *Saint Joan*
(1957), in which the heroine's hair was short
for historical realism. In *Breathless*, it is defiantly
modern, almost political, giving the actress
a distinctly androgynous look. In an era of
lacquered, carefully constructed hairstyles
for women, Seberg's short-haired beauty created
a sensation.

Eight years later Vidal Sassoon cut
Mia Farrow's hair short, live on US TV, for the
filming of *Rosemary's Baby*.

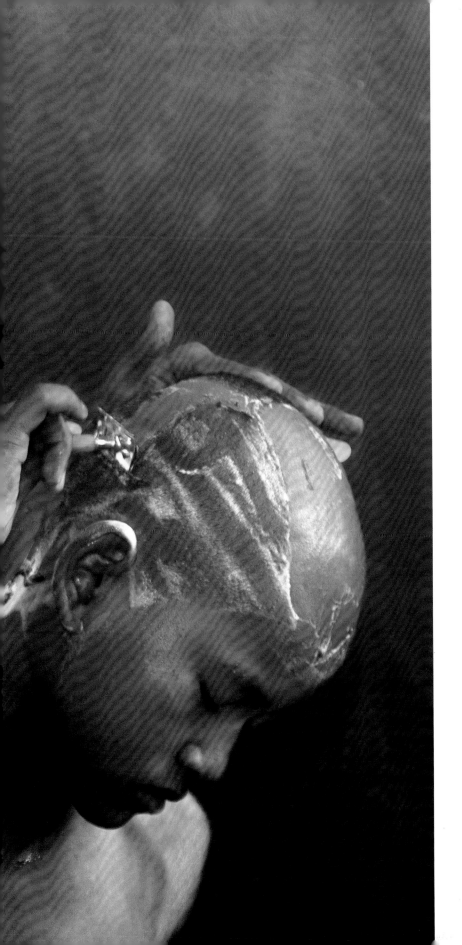

LEFT
Burmese Buddhist
novice monks have their
heads shaved, in keeping
with their religious voca-
tion. Symbolically there
is nothing between them
and their deities. Photo
Suzi Moore McGregor
2011

OPPOSITE
Skinheads belong to an urban tribe that started
in London in the 1960s. At first through music
and fashion they were associated with the Mods
(their name was derived from 'modernists' and
the 1950s modern jazz scene). By the 1970s
skinheads were more aligned with attitudes of
working-class rebellion, anarchy and the punk
movement. Photo Stuart Nicol
1980

RIGHT
Patti Smith. Photo Robert
Mapplethorpe
1978

FOLLOWING PAGES
*Jean-Louis David cuts Eva
M's hair.* Photo Helmut
Newton Paris
1974

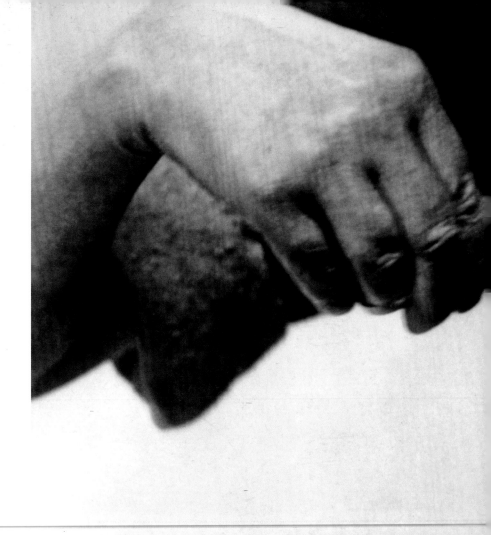

RIGHT
Maria Falconetti in the title
rôle in *La Passion de Jeanne
d'Arc* (The Passion of Joan
of Arc), 1928.

Joan symbolically and
publicly demonstrated
her personal sacrifice by
cutting her hair short
before she led the
Dauphin's army into battle
against the English.

Before her execution,
Joan's hair is forcibly cut
off once again.

Director Carl Theodor
Dreyer ordered Falconetti's
real hair to be cut off
on set, as the film rolled.
Members of the film
crew watched and wept.

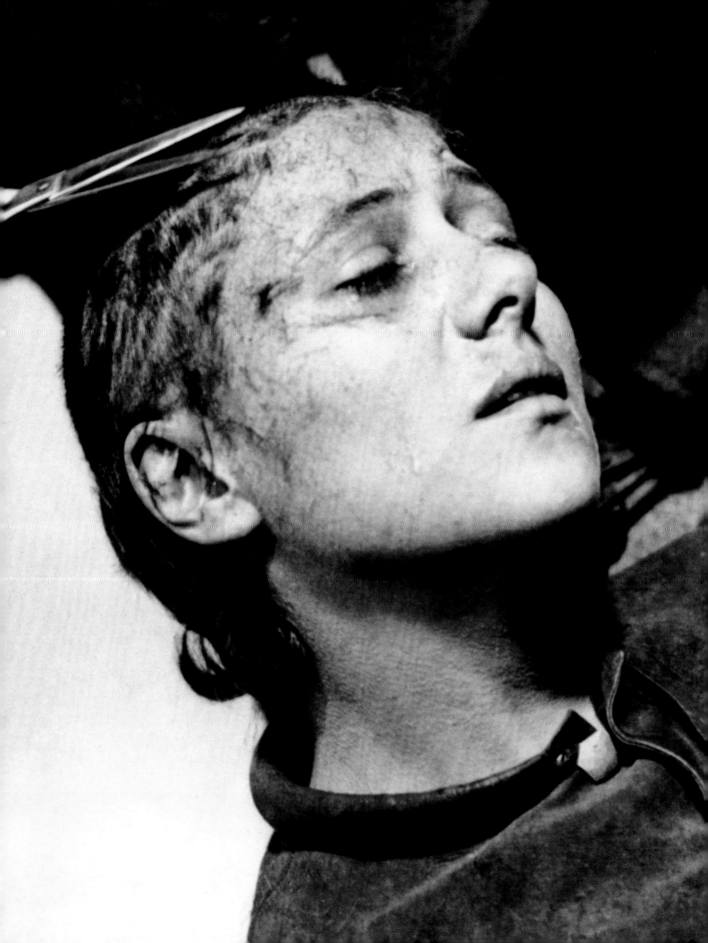

THE GRADUATED BOB

Top salon stylist Howard McLaren had no idea that this image by Michael Gordon, founder of New York salon Bumble and bumble, would become so iconic.

'I never planned the haircut,' said Howard McLaren. 'It was the right moment and it all came together. I created the cut based on classic British technique (Vidal Sassoon) and the elegance of French hairdressing (Antoine).

'*Vogue* was the first to feature the cut and it became very popular. It still is today because it's both masculine and feminine. The graduated bob is now a classic at the Bumble and bumble University.' It's still one of the most regularly taught cuts at the University and most frequently requested at the Bumble and bumble salons.

'I was taught to do technically perfect haircuts but not how to use my aesthetic. There was no technique for the razor, so I had to use my eye instead. The razor had been banished from hairdressing because it could be very destructive but for me there was a lot I couldn't do with just scissors.

'Living and working with magazines in Paris is where I developed the love of hairdressing and started to use a razor to replace my scissors.'

Photo Michael Gordon, 1988

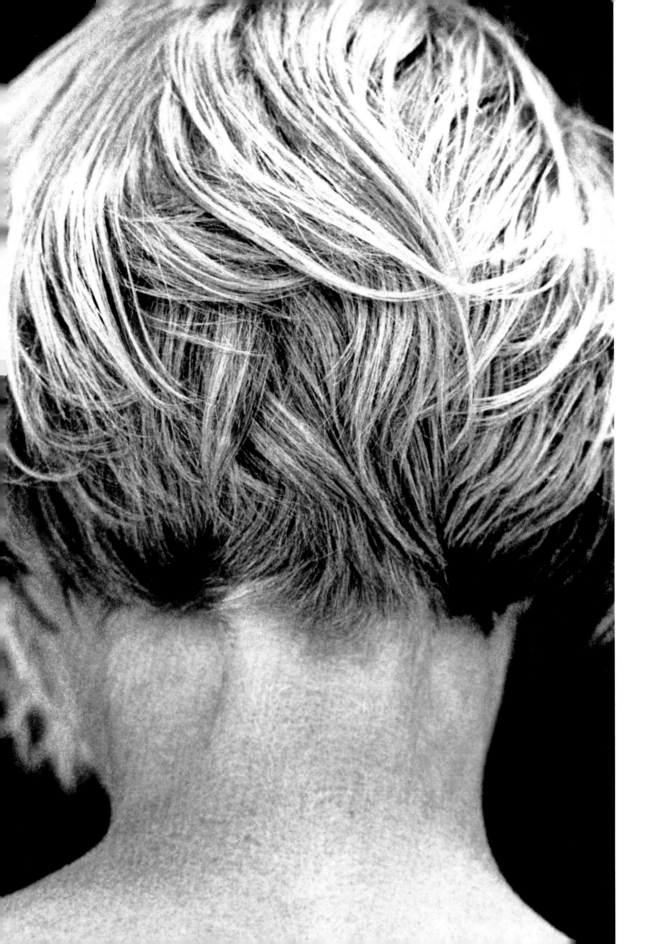

ABOVE
Hair by Laurent Philippon.
Photo Claudia Knoepfel
and Stefan Indlekofer
2011

OPPOSITE
Linda Evangelista rose to fame in the 1980s as
one of the fashion world's most in-demand models.
　　After she first agreed to have her hair cut short
by Julien d'Ys, her career entered the stratosphere.
　　Linda Evangelista is especially associated
with the notorious statement made about her
fellow supermodels, 'We don't get out of bed for
less than $10,000 a day'. Photo Patrick Demarchelier
1990

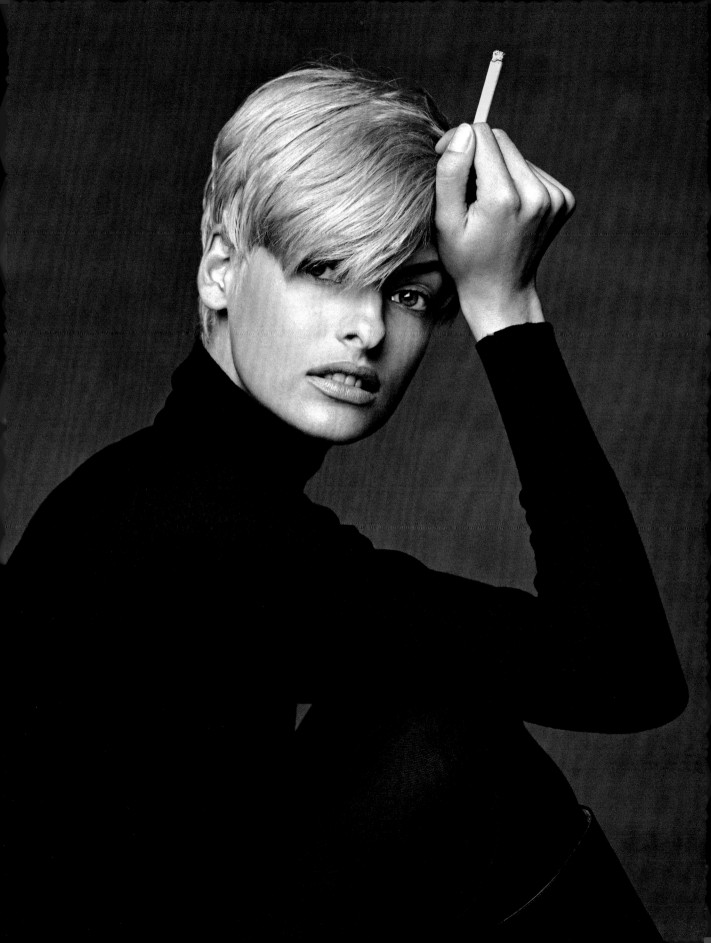

ABOVE
Hair by Maurice et
Gérard. Perfectionists and
innovators influenced
by Vidal Sassoon, they
created a cutting technique
in the 1980s they called
'pluriform' that allows
three different hair
shapes from a single cut.
Photo Gérard
1985

OPPOSITE
Raquel Zimmermann.
Hair by Laurent Philippon.
Photo Guy Aroch
2001

Laurent Philippon
meets Vidal Sassoon

THE ARCHITECTURE
OF HAIR

OPPOSITE
Hair by Vidal
Sassoon.
Photo Andreas
Heumann
1974

Short hair was part of women's liberation. It started in the 1920s with the 'flapper' look. Women had marvellous looks and great clothes then, but they didn't know how to cut their hair. When women started to have jobs they needed hair to suit their new lifestyle.

Alexandre taught so many people how to do his creative styles. Chignons are still done today – no one could do it like him – but even the best chignon is not easy to maintain. Women would sleep with it like Japanese geishas do.

I learned cutting hair with Raymond, Mr Teasie Weasie, in the early 1950s in London. He did everything with scissors only: he could shape hair, thin it without any thinning shears, no razors. When I opened my salon in 1954 on Bond Street I wanted to start something new. The first time we had total control over our scissors was in the 1960s, creating angles, geometry, asymmetry – all those things came from the knowledge we had of our scissors. We would train all night long! We said 'we won't backcomb your hair,

we won't tease it, we won't lacquer it – we are going to cut it to your bone structure.'

We were part of a revolution. We had to bring hairstyles up-to-date, like clothes and architecture. I was fascinated by architecture (Chicago's Michigan Avenue, Frank Lloyd Wright, Le Corbusier, Frank Gehry, Marcel Breuer). All those new shapes were so simple and so appealing to me. It is the prime art: sculpture comes from architecture. We were looking at hair like architects, studying a woman's face and figuring out which angles would suit her best.

Of course, there was opposition at first. It takes two years for the eye to get used to a new shape. But then being part of that change was tremendously exciting. Hairstyles were for everyone, even people who had never been in a hair salon before: a shop girl or a nurse could save a few shillings per month and come every four or five weeks and get a great haircut, and all they had to do was shampoo and condition, and let it swing.

OPPOSITE
Hair by Darryll at
Vidal Sassoon.
Photo Patrick Hunt
1972

People used to say, 'You're making young beautiful girls look like boys!' But some of the criticism came from other hairdressers. They said, 'Our customers have been coming every week for their shampoo and set, and now they'll only come once a month.' I told them, now many more women will come to your salon.

Working with photographers was a big part of my work. It is the only way you get talked about. Bailey, Donovan, Norman Parkinson in London and Avedon and Irving Penn in New York, Guy Bourdin in Paris…

The first fashion show we did was for Emmanuelle Khanh in Paris. We gave all the models haircuts, the Paris press went crazy, they loved it.

You can't have a revolution every ten years, but when you create something and you see it being taken somewhere further, that's evolution. In 1964 we created the 'five-point cut' on Grace Coddington, revealing the neckline, which was new at the time – fashion magazines from all over the world were raving about it.

I don't think you ever do it all. One would think that it's all been done but there is always an intuitive mind that will come and change things. I have trust in human ingenuity.

OPPOSITE
Grace Jones. Hair
by Laurent Philippon.
Photo Jean-Paul Goude
2009

FOLLOWING PAGES
Backstage at Isabelle
Ballu's couture show
'La Beauté Encadrée',
autumn/winter 1999–
2000. Hair by Laurent
Philippon. Photo Michael
Gordon
1999

CREDITS

2
Photo © Pierre et Gilles 1992
model: **Julie Delpy**; hair: **Laurent Philippon**;
make-up: **Midoriko**; stylist: **Odilon V. Ladeira**

8
Photo © Cédric Dordevic 1991
**Laurent Philippon, Alexandre de Paris,
Laetitia Scherrer**

4–5
Photo Thomas McAvoy
Time & Life Pictures/Getty Images

12–13
Photo © Jean-Paul Goude
models: **Marc Jacobs, Laurent Philippon,
Naomi Campbell**; hair: **Laurent Philippon**;
make-up: **Deedee Dorzee**; stylist: **Katie Grand**;
publication: *Harper's Bazaar* September 2007

6
Photo © Norbert Schoerner
model: **Julia Stegner**; hair: **Laurent Philippon**;
make-up: **Rie Omoto**; stylist: **Charlotte
Stockdale**; publication: *Vogue* UK June 2007

14
left © Rob Howard/Corbis
top right Photo W. Gellet, *The Graphic* 1912
bottom right © Tiziana and Gianni
Baldizzone/Corbis

16–17
16. Photo © Nickolas Muray 1938
Sipa Press/Rex Features
17. Photo © Mote Sinabel Aoki

18–19
18. **top right** Bob Marley, 1979
Photo Kirk West/Getty Images
bottom left Photo of a wheat paste in
Atlanta, Georgia © Mike Germon 2010
bottom right *Barcelona Grafica* 1930
19. **top left** from Ambroise Croizat,
*Traité complet et illustré de l'ondulation
artificielle des cheveux*
© INHA, Dist. RMN-Grand Palais/
Martine Beck-Coppola
top right Corbis/SuperStock
bottom The Royal Collection, 2011
Her Majesty Queen Elizabeth II/
Bridgeman Art Library

20–21
20. Photo © Prabuddha Dasgupta
model: **Lakshmi Menon**; hair: **Deepa Verma**;
make-up: **Deepa Verma**; publication:
Vogue India October 2007
21. Hotel Kanaga, Mopti, Mali
Photo © Thierry Mugler November 1989
models: **Katoucha Niane, Djimon Hounsou**;
hair: **Sally**; make-up: **Gael**

22–23
22. **top** From *A Journal of a Tour in the
Congo Free State* by Marcus R. P. Dorman,
Brussels and London 1905
bottom Photo © Cédric Dordevic 2010
23. **top left** © Nathaniel Welch/Corbis Outline
top right © So Yoon Lym, from the series
'The Dreamtime'. Clockwise from top left:
Jose, James, Jhonathan, Mario. 2009/2010.
Acrylic on paper. www.soyoonlym.com
bottom 19th-century engraving

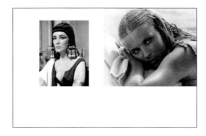

24–25
24. Elizabeth Taylor in *Cleopatra*, director
Joseph L. Mankiewicz 1963. 20th Century
Fox/Kobal Collection
hair: **Alexandre de Paris;** make-up:
Alberto de Rossi; stylist: **Renié**
25. Bo Derek in *10*, director Blake Edwards 1979
Photo Bruce McBroom
Licensed by Warner Bros. Entertainment Inc.
All Rights Reserved
hair: **Mary Keats;** make-up: **Ben Nye Jr;** stylist:
Patricia Edwards

26
Photo © David Marvier 2011
model: **Hilde;** hair: **Laurent Philippon;**
make-up: **Charlotte Le Clerre**

29
Photo © Norbert Schoerner
model: **Julia Stegner;** hair: **Laurent Philippon;**
make-up: **Rie Omoto;** stylist: **Charlotte
Stockdale;** publication: *Vogue* UK June 2007

30
Médulla (CD cover)
© 2004 Inez van Lamsweerde & Vinoodh Matadin
model: **Björk;** hair: **Hrafnhildur Arnardóttir;**
make-up: **Andrea Helgadóttir;** artwork (design):
M/M Paris

33
Médulla (CD cover)
© 2004 Inez van Lamsweerde & Vinoodh Matadin
model: **Björk;** hair: **Hrafnhildur Arnardóttir;**
make-up: **Andrea Helgadóttir;** artwork (design):
M/M Paris

35
Photo Richard Avedon
15 April 1968
© The Richard Avedon Foundation
model: **Twiggy;** hair: **Ara Gallant;**
Dress by Grès; publication: *Vogue* UK

37
Untitled no. 25
© RongRong & Inri 2008

38–39
38. *The Birthday Party.* Series Untitled #37
Photo © Vee Speers 2007
39. Photo © Cédric Buchet
model: **Laetitia Casta**; hair: **Laurent Philippon**;
make-up: **Karim Rahman**; stylist: **Anastasia
Barbieri**; publication: *Vogue Paris* January 2010

40
Alicia Keys 2002
Photo Paul Bergen/Redferns
hair: **Nikki Tucker**

42–43
42. Photo © Thiemo Sander
model: **Talytha**; hair: **Laurent Philippon**;
make-up: **Tracey Gray**; stylist: **Iain R. Webb**;
publication: *Elle* magazine May 2001
43. Photo © Thomas Schenk
model: **Vlada Roslyakova**; hair: **Laurent
Philippon**; make-up: **Vanessa McKenna**;
stylist: **Joanne Blades**; publication: *Vogue
Japan* autumn-winter 2005/6

45
Photo © Richard Bush
model: **Lesly Masson**; hair: **Eugene Souleiman**;
make-up: **Makky P**; stylist: **Charles Varenne**;
publication: *Numéro* magazine 2005

46–47
Photo © David LaChapelle,
Hippie Story: Black Panther
model: **Grace Kelsey**; hair: **Laurent Philippon**;
publication: *The Face* April 2002

48
top left Private Collection
Photo Agnew's, London/Bridgeman Art Library
top right Fox Photos/Hulton Archive/
Getty Images
bottom United Artists/Kobal Collection/
St. Hilaire, AL

50–51
50. *Gilda*, director Charles Vidor 1946
Columbia/Kobal Collection/Bob Coburn
model: Rita Hayworth; hair: Helen Hunt;
make-up: Clay Campbell; stylist: Jean-Louis
51. Photo Jacques-Henri Lartigue 1931
model: Renée Perle

52–53
52. **top left** Marisa Berenson in *Barry Lyndon*,
director Stanley Kubrick, 1975
hair: wig by Leonard of Mayfair (Leonard Lewis);
make-up: Alan Boyle; stylist: Milena Canonero
top right Paolo Veronese, *The Mystic
Marriage of St Catherine* (detail), c. 1575

bottom left Elizabeth Taylor and Alexandre de Paris
bottom right Alison Arngrim as Nellie Oleson, *Little
House on the Prairie*. Photo Patrick Loubatière
53. **top left** Photo DeAgostini/Getty Images
top right from Ambroise Croizat, *Traité complet
et illustré de l'ondulation artificielle des cheveux*
bottom *Bride of Frankenstein*, Photo James Whale
1935. Universal/The Kobal Collection/Roman Freulich
model: Elsa Lanchester; hair: Irma Kusely; make-up:
Jack P. Pierce

54–55
© Estate Brassaï – RMN-Grand Palais
Photo RMN/Jean-Gilles Berizzi

56–57
56. Ona Munson as 'Mother' Gin Sling
in *The Shanghai Gesture*, director Josef von
Sternberg 1941 © rue des Archives/BCA
hair: Hazel Rogers; make-up: Bob Stephanoff;
stylist: Royer
57. Photo George Hoyningen-Huene © *Vogue* Paris
'Elizabeth Arden sculptured head', jewels by Boucheron
Vogue Paris July 1932
model: Dolores Wilkinson; hair: Antoine

59
Pam Grier in *Foxy Brown*,
director Jack Hill 1974
The Kobal Collection
stylist: **Ruthie West**

65
Photo © Sølve Sundsbø/Art + Commerce
model: **Katrin Thormann**; hair: **Laurent Philippon**;
make-up: **Peter Philips**; stylist: **Marie Chaix**;
publication: *Vogue* Germany September 2009

60–61
60. Photo © Max Vadukul
model: **Shalom Harlow**; hair: **Yannick d'Is**;
make-up: **Thierry Mauduit**; stylist: **Nicoletta Santoro**;
publication: *Vogue* France 1993
61. Photo © Claudia Knoepfel and Stefan Indlekofer
model: **Julia Stegner**; hair: **Laurent Philippon**;
make-up: **Christelle Cocquet**; stylist: **Nicola Knels**;
publication: *Vogue* Germany December 2010

66–67
Photo © David LaChapelle
Dear Doctor, I've Read Your Play
model: **Polina Kouklina**; hair: **Laurent Philippon**;
make-up: **Petros Petrohilos**; stylist: **Nicoletta
Santoro**; publication: *Vogue* Italia October 2004

62
Photo © Ali Mahdavi 2012
model: **Dita Von Teese**; hair: **Laurent Philippon**;
make-up: **Lloyd Simmonds**; stylist: **Suzanne
von Aichinger**

68–69
68. Photo © Cédric Buchet
models: **Eva Herzigova, Betsy Miller**; hair: **Laurent
Philippon**; make-up: **Franck B**; stylist: **Sophia
Neophitou**; publication: *10 magazine*, autumn 2008
69. Photo © Greg Kadel/Trunk Archive
model: **Elin Skoghagen**; hair: **Eugene Souleiman**;
make-up: **Alex Box**; stylist: **Patti Wilson**;
publication: *Vogue* Italia November 2006

70–71
Photo © Craig McDean/Art + Commerce
hair: Orlando Pita; make-up: Peter Philips;
stylist: **Phyllis Posnick**; publication: *Vogue* US
January 2005

77
Photo Franco Rubartelli
© Condé Nast Archive/Corbis
model: Veruschka; hair: Alba e Francesca;
publication: *Vogue* April 1969

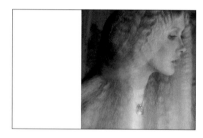

72–73
Photo Barry Lategan/*Vogue*
© The Condé Nast Publications Ltd
hair: **John at Leonard of Mayfair**;
make-up: **Barbara Daly**; publication: *Vogue* UK
February 1975

79
Photo © Bojana Tatarska 2011
model: Alex Yuryeva; hair: Laurent Philippon;
make-up: Kader; stylist: Laurent Philippon

74–75
Photo Barry Lategan/*Vogue*
© The Condé Nast Publications Ltd
publication: *Vogue* UK July 1972

80–81
Photo © Terry Richardson/Art Partner
model: Lara Stone; hair: Laurent Philippon;
make-up: Romy Souleimani; stylist: Carine Roitfeld;
publication: *Vogue Hommes* 2008–2009

82
top left © rue des Archives / Keystone Zurich
top right Private Collection/Giraudon/
Bridgeman Art Library
bottom Photo *Evening Standard/*
Hulton Archive/Getty Images

84–85
84. **top** Photo Scala, Florence
bottom left Carole Bouquet
For Your Eyes Only, 1981
hair: Stephanie Kaye; make-up: Eric Allwright;
stylist: Elizabeth Waller
bottom right Photo © Theo van Houts 1968
85. IAM/akg-images

86–87
Wuthering Heights
Photo © Duane Michals
model: Angela Lindvall; hair: Laurent Philippon;
stylist: Emmanuelle Alt; publication: *Mixte*
magazine (no. 9) spring 2000

89
Photo © Bruce McBroom 1976
model: Farrah Fawcett; hair: Allen Edwards

90–91
Jesus is My Homeboy
Photo David LaChapelle 2003

93
Photo Richard Avedon
© The Richard Avedon Foundation
model: Nadja Auermann; hair: Yannick d'Is;
publication: Pirelli Calendar 1995

94–95
94. Photo © Mark Segal
model: Vlada Roslyakova; hair: Laurent Philippon;
make-up: Aaron de Mey; stylist: Julia von Boehm;
publication: *Vogue* France January 2008
95. Photo © Anthony Maule
model: Eniko Mihalik; hair: Laurent Philippon;
make-up: Lloyd Simmonds; stylist: Samuel François;
publication: *Numéro* magazine September 2011

100–101
Photo Patrick Hunt/*Vogue*
© The Condé Nast Publications Ltd
publication: *Vogue Beauty* summer 1973

102
Photo © Corinne Day/Trunk Archive
model: Kate Moss; hair: Drew Jarrett; stylist:
Melanie Ward; publication: *The Face* 1990

96–97
Photo Franco Rubartelli
© Condé Nast Archive/Corbis
model: Veruschka; hair: Ara Gallant;
publication: *Vogue* 1966

104–105
104. Photo © Serge Leblon
model: Charlotte Gainsbourg; hair:
Laurent Philippon; make-up: Max Delorme;
stylist: Julia von Boehm; publication:
Double magazine 2004
105. Photo © Nan Goldin 2000
model: Joana Preiss

99
Photo © Sofia Sanchez & Mauro Mongellio
model: Evelina Mambetova at Silent Models NY;
hair: Laurent Philippon; make-up: Lloyd
Simmonds; stylist: Samuel François;
publication: *Numéro* magazine November 2008

107
Photo © David Marvier
model: **Salomé Jugeli**; hair: **Laurent Philippon**;
make-up: **Christelle Cocquet**; stylist: **Laurent
Philippon**; publication: *Virgine* magazine 2011

113
Photo © Cédric Buchet
model: **Alla Kostromichova**; hair: **Laurent Philippon**;
make-up: **Maki Ryoke**; publication: *Bergdorf
Goodman* magazine autumn 2009–10

108–109
108. Photo © Herlinde Koelbl Focus/Cosmos 2007
109. *Shirin Neshat – Identified*, 1995
B&W RC print & ink (photo taken by Cynthia Preston)
© Shirin Neshat Courtesy Gladstone Gallery,
New York and Brussels

114
Photo © Prabuddha Dasgupta
model: **Lakshmi Menon**; hair: **Laurent Philippon**;
make-up: **Christelle Cocquet**; publication: **Ritu Kumar**
fall 2009/winter 2010

110–111
Photo Franco Rubartelli
© Condé Nast Archive/Corbis
model: **Veruschka**; publication: *Vogue* June 1968

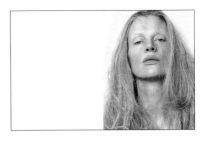

117
Photo © Philip Riches 2010
model: **Kristen McMenamy**

118
Recluse
Photo © Alex Stoddard March 2012
model: Victoria Robbins

124
top Galleria degli Uffizi, Florence
centre left Cesare Vecellio,
Venetian lady bleaching her hair, c. 1590
centre middle Nicholas Hilliard,
Marguerite de Valois, Queen of Navarre, 1577
centre right John Malkovich in *Dangerous Liaisons*,
director Stephen Frears 1988
Collection Christophel © Etienne George
Wig by Peter Owen; make-up: Jean-Luc Russier;
stylist: James Acheson
bottom *Wild at Heart*, director David Lynch 1990
model: Isabella Rossellini; hair: Frida Aradottir;
make-up: Michelle Bühler; stylist: Amy Stofsky

121
Photo © Mark Segal
model: Vlada Roslyakova; hair: Laurent Philippon;
make-up: Aaron de Mey; stylist: Julia von Boehm;
publication: *Vogue* France January 2008

128–129
128. Jean Harlow, 25 June 1933
Photo Keystone/Hulton Archive/Getty Images
129. *Hollywood Killer Wave* © Stefano Canulli 2013

122–123
Photo © David LaChapelle, *No Doubt*
video stills: *It's My Life*
model: Gwen Stefani; hair: Laurent Philippon;
make-up: Scott Barnes; stylist: Andrea Lieberman

130–131
130. **top left** © Condé Nast Archive/Corbis
bottom left Photo Marisa Rastellini/Mondadori
Portfolio via Getty Images
top right © Condé Nast Archive/Corbis
bottom right Photo Silver Screen
Collection/Moviepix/Getty Images
131. Photo Nigel Dobinson/Hulton Archive/
Getty Images

134–135
134. Photo © Marc Hispard
model: Claudia Schiffer; hair: Laurent Philippon;
make-up: Patty Dubroff; stylist: Marie-Amélie Sauvé;
publication: *Vogue* France January 1995
135. Photo © Jan Welters
model: Saskia de Brauw; hair: Laurent Philippon;
make-up: Christine Corbel; stylist: Jos van Heel;
publication: *Vogue* Netherlands October 2012

132–133
132. *Palm Springs, California*
Photo © Robert Doisneau 1960
133. Photo © Mario Testino/Art Partner
model: Meghan Douglas; hair: Laurent Philippon;
make-up: Tom Pecheux; stylist: Lucinda Chambers;
publication: *Vogue* UK February 1995

137
Photo © Paola Kudacki/Trunk Archive
model: Aline Weber; hair: Laurent Philippon;
make-up: Lloyd Simmonds; stylist: Melanie Huynh;
publication: *Vogue* France November 2008

138–139
Photo © Bryan Adams
model: **Daphne Guinness**; wig by **Laurent
Philippon**, hair by **Tyler Johnston**; make-up:
Phyllis Cohen; stylist: **Lotta Aspenberg**;
publication: *Zoo magazine September 2010*

145
The Twins
Photo © Sebastian Kim
model: **Ginta Lapina and Andrej Pejić**;
hair: **Laurent Philippon**; make-up:
Maud Laceppe; stylist: **Charles Varenne**;
publication: *Numéro* magazine November 2011

141
Photo © Herb Ritts/Trunk Archive
model: **Alek Wek**; hair: **Peter Savic**;
stylist: **Marcus von Ackermann**; dress by **Chloé**;
publication: *Vogue France April 1999*

146–147
146. Cyndi Lauper
Photo © Gary Lewis 1984
147. Photo © Karl Lagerfeld
model: **Raquel Zimmermann**; hair: **Laurent Philippon**;
make-up: **James Kaliardos**; stylist: **Charlotte Stockdale**;
publication: *V magazine winter 2008/9*

142
Photo © François Nars
model: **Daphne Guinness**; hair: **Peter Gray**;
make-up: **Lena Koro**; stylist: **Patti Wilson**;
publication: *Nars 15/15 2009*

149
Self-portrait
Photo © Karl Lagerfeld 2012

150
Photo © Craig McDean/Art + Commerce
model: **Tilda Swinton**; hair: **Sam McKnight**;
make-up: **Lucia Pieroni**; stylist: **Edward Enninful**
and **Jerry Stafford**; publication: *i-D* magazine 2003

156–157
Personal notebook © Julien d'Ys, March 2009
for Comme des Garçons autumn/winter 2010
collection
Photo © Ilker Akyol
model: **Sharon and Amanda**; head stylist: **Julien d'Ys**

152
Photos © David LaChapelle 2003
model: **Amanda Lepore**; hair: **Laurent Philippon**

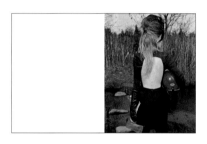

159
Photo © Jennifer Tzar
model: **Julie**; hair: **Laurent Philippon**;
make-up: **Regina Harris**, stylist: **Patti Wilson**,
publication: *Tank* magazine 2005

154–155
Photo © Luciana Val and Franco Musso
model: **Giedre Dukauskaite**; hair: **Laurent Philippon**;
make-up: **Lloyd Simmonds**; stylist: **Capucine Safyurtlu**;
publication: *Numéro* magazine November 2007

160–161
Die Antwoord (Yolandi and Ninja).
Photo Sebastian Kim 2010
publication: *Interview* magazine

162
top left © Hei Yue, Beijing, 2005
Courtesy of Hei Yue Galerie Paris–Beijing
top right Scody, Crass, Paris 1988.
Ralf Marsault & Heino Muller, 25/34 Photographes
Photo © Ralf Marsault & Heino Muller
bottom DeAgostini/Scala, Florence

166–167
166. **left** The Granger Collection/TopFoto
top right Benjamin A. Gifford Photographs
(P218-SG 1), Special Collections & Archives
Research Center, OSU Libraries, Corvallis, Oregon
bottom right Photo Edward S. Curtis/
George Eastman House/Getty Images
167. Library of Congress, Prints & Photographs Division,
Edward S. Curtis Collection, reproduction number
LC-USZ62-98534, Washington, DC

164–165
164. 'Coiffure Mutussi – Ruanda'
Photo 1923 Collection Pierre Loos, Brussels
All rights reserved
165. **top left** © RMN-Grand Palais
(Musée du Louvre)/Franck Raux
top right Musée du quai Branly/Scala, Florence
bottom Baga, Guinea. Private Collection
© Archives Musée Dapper et Hughes Dubois

169
Magnum/Robert Capa © International
Center of Photography

170
Photo LNA/*Evening Standard*/
Hulton Archive/Getty Images

173
Photo © Ted Polhemus
Pymca Images

174
Photo © Adrian Wilson
April 2009
model: Alice Dellal

177
Photo © Carl W. Heindl 2009

179
Pink Flamingos, director John Waters 1972
Collection Christophel
© Dreamland Divine
hair: David Lochary and Mink Stole; make-up:
Van Smith; stylist: Van Smith

181
© Martin Parr/Magnum Photos

183
Subway, director Luc Besson 1985
Isabelle Adjani; hair: Isabelle Gamsohn;
make-up: Maud Baron; stylist: Martine Rapin

184
Photo © Mario Testino/Art Partner
model: Kate Moss; hair: Orlando Pita; make-up:
Tom Pecheux; publication: *The Face* May 1996

188
Photo © Paolo Roversi/Art + Commerce
model: Othilia Simon; hair: Sam McKnight;
make-up: Hannah Murray; stylist: Lucinda Chambers;
publication: *Vogue* UK September 2010

186–187
186. Photo © Anthony Maule
model: Aymeline Valade; hair: Laurent
Philippon; make-up: Lloyd Simmonds;
stylist: Samuel François; publication: *Numéro
magazine* March 2011
187. Photo © Ben Hassett
model: Maggie Rizer; hair: Laurent Philippon;
make-up: Stephanie Kunz; stylist: Julia von
Boehm; publication: *Vogue* Japan July 2007

191
Photo © David Marvier
model: Salomé Jugeli; hair: Laurent Philippon;
make-up: Christelle Cocquet; stylist: Laurent
Philippon; publication: *Virgine magazine* 2011

192
Photo © Joe Lally
model: Molly Gunn; hair: Laurent Philippon;
make-up: Angie Parker; stylist: Patti Wilson;
publication: *Tokion* September 2006

194–195
194. © Martin Parr/Magnum Photos 1997
195. Photo © Sofia Sanchez and Mauro Mongiello
model: **Katlin Aas**; hair: **Laurent Philippon**;
make-up: **Lloyd Simmonds**; stylist: **Samuel François**;
publication: *Numéro* magazine September 2009

200
top left RMN-Grand Palais
(Musee du Louvre)/Thierry Le Mage
top right Pellegrini Chapel, Verona
bottom Photo Leemage Collection/
Universal Images Group/Getty Images

197
Los Angeles 2019
Photo © Craig McDean/Art + Commerce
model: **Natasha Poly**; hair: **Orlando Pita**;
make-up: **Peter Philips**; stylist: **Carine Roitfeld**;
publication: *Vogue* Paris June/July 2004

203
© Alexandre de Paris

204
Photo Ronald Traeger/*Vogue*
© The Condé Nast Publications Ltd
publication: *Vogue* UK April 1967

198–199
Photo © Jerry Schatzberg/Trunk Archive
model: **Sarah Thom**

207
Photo Richard Avedon August 1965
© Richard Avedon Foundation
model: **Jean Shrimpton**; hair: **Alexandre de Paris**

213
Photo © David Marvier
model: **Salomé Jugeli**; hair: **Laurent Philippon**;
make-up: **Christelle Cocquet**; stylist: **Laurent
Philippon**; publication: *Virgine* magazine 2011

209
Homage to *The Shanghai Gesture*
Photo © Ali Mahdavi 2001
model: **Carrie Perrodo**; hair: **Laurent Philippon**;
make-up: **Tania Gandre**

214
Photo © The Estate of Jeanloup Sieff
model: **Lucie de la Falaise**; hair: **Laurent Philippon**;
make-up: **Terry**; publication: *Elle* UK 1990

211
Photo © Annie Leibovitz 2008
model: **Julien d'Ys and Raquel Zimmermann**;
head stylist: **Julien d'Ys**

217
Photo © Anthony Maule
model: **Catherine McNeil**; hair: **Laurent Philippon**;
make-up: **Lloyd Simmonds**; stylist: **Samuel François**;
publication: *Numéro* magazine November 2010

218–219
218. Photo © Alex Cayley
model: Querelle Jansen; hair: Laurent Philippon;
make-up: Mary Jane Frost; stylist: Patti Wilson;
publication: *Vogue* Italia December 2004
219. Lucasfilm/The Kobal Collection
hair: Sue Love; make-up: Paul Engelen;
stylist: Trisha Biggar

224–225
224. Photo © Regan Cameron
model: Stella Tennant; hair: Laurent Philippon;
make-up: Lisa Eldridge; stylist: Jayne Pickering;
publication: *Vogue* January 1997
225. Photo © Ali Mahdavi
model: Marcelle Bittar; hair: Laurent Philippon;
make-up: Lloyd Simmonds; stylist: Catherine Baba;
publication: *Tank* magazine 2006

221
Julien d'Ys' personal notebook
Photo © Patrick Demarchelier
model: Karlie Kloss; head stylist:
Julien d'Ys; stylist: Phyllis Posnick;
publication: *Vogue* November 2009

226 227
226. Photo © Bojana Tatarska 2011
model: Alex Yuryeva; hair: Laurent Philippon;
make-up: Kader; stylist: Laurent Philippon
227. Photo © Richard Burbridge
model: Vlada Roslyakova; hair: Laurent Philippon;
make-up: Ellis Faas; stylist: Robbie Spencer;
publication: *Dazed & Confused* April 2012

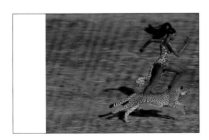

223
Photo © Jean-Paul Goude
model: Naomi Campbell; hair: Laurent Philippon;
make-up: Lloyd Simmonds; stylist: Alex Aikiu;
publication: *Harper's Bazaar* September 2009

229
Photo © Jacqueline Di Milia/Corbis Outline

230
Photo © Richard Burbridge 2006
model: Irina Lazareanu; hair: Laurent Philippon;
make-up: Inge Grognard; stylist: Joanne Blades

232
top left © Gerard Degeorge/Bridgeman Art Library
top right White Images/Scala, Florence
bottom *Il Casanova di Federico Fellini*, director
Federico Fellini 1976; hair: Gabriella Borzelli;
make-up: Rino Carboni; stylist: Danilo Donati

234–235
234. **left** Léonard Autié
top right 'The vis-à-vis bisected or the Ladies Corp',
1776. Caricatures collected by Horace Walpole.
Miriam and Ira D. Wallach Division of Art, Prints and
Photographs, New York Public Library, Astor, Lenox &
Tilden Foundation

bottom right Photo Art Media/Heritage Images/
Scala, Florence
235. **top left** © Roger-Viollet/TopFoto
bottom left Antoine, *Document sur la Coiffure*
right Israel Museum, Jerusalem/Vera & Arturo
Schwarz Collection of Dada and Surrealist Art/
Bridgeman Art Library

237
© Horace Bristol/Corbis

238–239
Wigs by Antoine de Paris, 1938

241
Photo © Jason Kibbler
model: Shu-Pei Qin; hair: James Pecis
make-up: Alice Lane; stylist: Olga Dunina,
dress by Dior; publication: *Vogue* Russia April 2013

242–243
Photo © David LaChapelle
model: **Daphne Guinness**; hair: **Laurent Philippon**;
make-up: **Sharon Gault**; stylist: **Daphne Guinness**;
publication: *Harper's Bazaar* China December 2002

249
Photo © Herb Ritts/Trunk Archive
model: **Helena Christensen**; hair: **Peter Savic**

244
Love Me
Photo © David LaChapelle
model: **Rie Rasmussen**; hair: **Laurent Philippon**;
make-up: **Justin Henry**; stylist: **Patti Wilson**;
publication: *Vogue* Italia May 2002

250-251
Photo © Kenneth Cappello
hair: **Nagi Noda**; stylist: **Cindy Greene**

247
Airbrushed Wings
Photo © David LaChapelle 2002
hair: **Laurent Philippon**

253
Photo © Miles Aldridge
model: **Ai Tominaga**; hair: **Laurent Philippon**;
make-up: **Lloyd Simmonds**; stylist: **Patti Wilson**;
publication: *Vogue* Italia September 2010

254–255
Comme des Garçons catwalk,
autumn/winter 2012–13
Photo © Ilker Akyol; head stylist: Julien d'Ys

260–261
Delpire Prods/The Kobal Collection
Who Are You, Polly Maggoo?,
director William Klein 1966
hair: Vidal Sassoon

256
Photo © Greg Lotus/Art + Commerce
hair: Laurent Philippon; make-up: Kabuki;
stylist: Sophia Neophitou; publication:
Vogue Italia February 2006

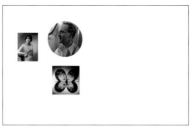

262
left © rue des Archives/René Dazy
top right Antoine de Paris
bottom right Sisters G., 1930
Photo Studio Manassé

259
Photo © Patrick Demarchelier
models: Mariacarla Boscono, Anja Rubik
hair: Laurent Philippon; make-up: Tom Pecheux;
stylist: Patti Wilson; publication: *Vogue* Italia
November 2008

265
Photo all rights reserved
Hair by Antoine de Paris

267
Moviestore Collection/Rex Features

274–275
Photo © The Helmut Newton Estate
hair: Jean-Louis David

268–269
Photo © Suzi Moore McGregor 2011

276–277
Maria Falconetti in *La Passion de Jeanne d'Arc*
(The Passion of Joan of Arc),
director Carl Theodor Dreyer 1928

271
Photo Stuart Nicol/Hulton Archive/Getty Images

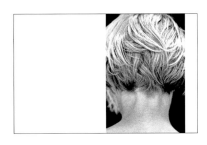

279
Photo © Michael Gordon
hair: Howard McLaren

273
Photo Robert Mapplethorpe
© Copyright the Robert Mapplethorpe Foundation.
Courtesy Art + Commerce

280–281
280. Photo © Claudia Knoepfel
and Stefan Indlekofer
model: Caroline Brasch Nielsen; hair: Laurent
Philippon; make-up: Christelle Cocquet;
stylist: Veronique Didry; publication: *Vogue*
Russia May 2011
281. Photo © Patrick Demarchelier
model: Linda Evangelista; publication: *Madame
Figaro* 1990

282–283
282. Photo © Guy Aroch/Trunk Archive
model: Raquel Zimmermann; hair: Laurent
Philippon; make-up: Pascale Guichard; stylist:
Laurence Alexandre; publication: *Elle* magazine
November 2001
283. Photo © Gérard 1985
hair: Maurice et Gérard

284
Nefertiti
Photo © Andreas Heumann
hair: Vidal Sassoon; publication: *Vogue UK April 1974*

287
Photo Patrick Hunt/*Vogue*
© The Condé Nast Publications Ltd
hair: Darryll at Vidal Sassoon; publication:
Vogue UK July 1972

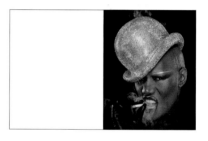

289
Photo © Jean-Paul Goude
model: Grace Jones; hair: Laurent Philippon;
make-up: Terry Barber; stylist: Alex Aikiu;
publication: *V magazine spring 2009*

290–291
Backstage at Isabelle Ballu autumn/winter
1999–2000 'La Beauté Encadrée'
Photo © Michael Gordon
hair: Laurent Philippon; make-up: Carole Lasnier;
stylist: Isabelle Ballu

COVER
Photo © Christophe Kutner
model: Rachel Kirby; hair: Laurent Philippon;
make-up: Carole Lasnier

ON THE CONTRIBUTORS

Natasha Fraser-Cavassoni (pp. 103, 171, 205) is a writer living in Paris.

Daphne Guinness (p. 143) is an artist and international fashion muse.

Yannick d'Is (p. 92) is a hairstylist living in Paris.

David LaChapelle (pp. 245–246) is an artist and photographer living in Los Angeles.

Stéphanie Laithier is senior lecturer in history at the Sorbonne, Paris.

Amanda Lepore (p. 153) is an artist and performer.

Sam McKnight (p. 189) is a hairstylist living In London.

Kathy Phillips (pp. 125–126) is International Beauty Director Conde Nast Asia Pacific.

Orlando Pita (p. 185) is a hairstylist living in New York.

Claudine Roméo (pp. 115–116) is senior lecturer in philosophy at the Sorbonne, Paris.

Vidal Sassoon (1928–2012) (pp. 285–286) was a British hairstylist.

Shoplifter (aka Hrafnhildur Arnardóttir) (pp. 31–32) is an Icelandic artist living in New York.

Eugene Souleiman (p. 45) is a hairstylist living in New York.

Nikki Tucker (p. 41) is a hairstylist living in Richmond, Virginia.

Veruschka (p. 110) is an actress and artist.

Dita Von Teese (p. 63) is a burlesque dancer and actress living in Los Angeles.

Patti Wilson (p. 58) is a fashion stylist living in New York.

Julien d'Ys (p. 221) is an artist and hairstylist living in Paris.

Ewa Ziembinska (p. 238) is a curator at the National Museum in Warsaw.

ACKNOWLEDGMENTS

I would like to extend my warmest thanks to all those who helped in the making of this book, most particularly:

Isabelle Adjani, Die Antwoord, Victor Audoin, Isabelle Ballu, Caroline Berton at *Vogue* Paris, Björk, Lucy Cox at *Vogue* UK, Brett Croft, Divine, Babeth Djian, Cédric Dordevic, Natasha Fraser-Cavassoni, Yann Gabin, Charlotte Gainsbourg, Michael Gordon, Daphne Guinness, Tim Howard, Marc Jacobs, Grace Jones, Alicia Keys, Floor Kleyne, Kumi Gena Tanimura, Virginie Laguens, Stéphanie Laithier, Cyndi Lauper, Caroline Lebar, Amanda Lepore, Tereza Le Fellic, Pierre Loos, Gabriel Lopes, Laurent Mercier (Lola), Toni Morris, Minako Norimatsu, Neil Moodie, Massimiliano Moretti, Jason Olson, Josephine Paterek, Lydia Philippon, Kathy Phillips, Jean-François Rafalli, Patrice Renard, Claudine Roméo, Jean Seberg, Michelle Service Fraccari, Patti Smith, Gwen Stefani, Tilda Swinton, Mark Szaszy, Dita Von Teese, Bénédicte de Valicourt, Veruschka, Melanie Ward, Patti Wilson, Amy Winehouse, Ewa Ziembinska

Hairdressers:
Alexandre de Paris, Antoine, Frida Aradottir, Gabriella Borzelli, Ara Gallant, Isabelle Gamsohn, Peter Gray, Helen Hunt, Yannick d'Is, Mary Keats, Irma Kusely, Léonard, David Lochary, Sue Love, Maurice et Gérard, Sam McKnight, Howard McLaren, Peter Owen, James Pecis, Orlando Pita, Hazel Rogers, Sally, Vidal Sassoon, Eugene Souleiman, Mink Stole, Nikki Tucker, Deepa Verma, Julien d'Ys

Photographers and artists:
Bryan Adams, Ilker Akyol, Miles Aldridge, Guy Aroch, Richard Avedon, Brassaï, Cédric Buchet, Richard Burbridge, Richard Bush, Regan Cameron, Stefano Canulli, Robert Capa, Kenneth Cappello, Alex Cayley, Christophe Kutner, Prabuddha Dasgupta, Corinne Day, Patrick Demarchelier, Robert Doisneau, Cédric Dordevic, Pierre et Gilles, Mike Germon, Nan Goldin, Michael Gordon, Jean-Paul Goude, Ben Hassett, Carl W. Heindl, Hei Yue, Jacques-Henri Lartigue, Andreas Heumann, Hei Yue, Marc Hispard, George Hoyningen-Huene, Patrick Hunt, Greg Kadel, Jason Kibbler, Sebastian Kim, William Klein, Claudia Knoepfel and Stefan Indlekofer, Herlinde Koelbl, Paola Kudacki, David LaChapelle, Karl Lagerfeld, Joe Lally, Barry Lategan, Serge Leblon, Annie Leibovitz, Gary Lewis, Greg Lotus, Ali Madhavi, Studio Manassé, Robert Mapplethorpe, Ralf Marsault, David Marvier, Anthony Maule, Bruce McBroom, Craig McDean, Suzi Moore McGregor, Duane Michals, Mote Sinabel Aoki, Thierry Mugler, Nagi Noda, François Nars, Shirin Neshat, Helmut Newton, Stuart Nicol, Martin Parr, Terry Richardson, Philip Riches, Herb Ritts, RongRong & Inri, Paolo Roversi, Franco Rubartelli, Sofia Sanchez and Mauro Mongellio, Thiemo Sanders, Jerry Schatzberg, Thomas Schenk, Norbert Schoerner, Mark Segal, Shoplifter, Jeanloup Sieff, So Yoon Lim, Vee Speers, Alex Stoddard,

Sølve Sundsbø, Bojana Tatarska, Mario Testino, Ronald Traeger, Jennifer Tzar, Nev Usumbra, Max Vadukul, Luciana Val and Franco Musso, Inez van Lamsweerde and Vinoodh Matadin, Theo van Houts, Jan Welters, Adrian Wilson

Models:
Veruschka, Katlin Aas, Nadja Auermann, Marisa Berenson, Marcelle Bittar, Mariacarla Boscono, Caroline Brasch Nielsen, Naomi Campbell, Laetitia Casta, Saskia de Brauw, Lucie de la Falaise, Alice Dellal, Julie Delpy, Meghan Douglas, Giedre Dukauskaite, Linda Evangelista, Molly Gunn, Shalom Harlow, Querelle Jansen, Salome Jugeli, Grace Kelsey, Karlie Kloss, Polina Kouklina, Alla Kostromichova, Ginta Lapina, Irina Lazareanu, Angela Lindvall, Evelina Mambetova, Kristen McMenamy, Catherine McNeil, Lakshmi Menon, Eniko Mihalik, Kate Moss, Andrej Pejić, Carrie Perrodo, Natasha Poly, Talytha Pugliesi, Maggie Rizer, Victoria Robbins, Vlada Roslyakova, Anja Rubik, Laetitia Scherrer, Claudia Schiffer, Jean Shrimpton, Shu-Pei Qin, Othilia Simon, Elin Skoghagen, Julia Stegner, Lara Stone, Stella Tennant, Katrin Thormann, Sarah Thom, Ai Tominaga, Aymeline Valade, Aline Weber, Alex Yuryeva, Raquel Zimmermann

Special thanks to:
Philip Watson and the Thames & Hudson team
Margaux Duroux, Virginie Schwob, Agnès Vergne
Hélène Orizet and Catherine Aygalinc
Peter Lichtenthal and Tim Rush at Bumble and bumble

INDEX

Now it's time to fly a kite. LP